P9-AFX-166

FOOD
EQUIPMENT
FACTS

641.57
S 434f

FOOD EQUIPMENT FACTS

A HANDBOOK
FOR THE
FOODSERVICE INDUSTRY

Revised
and
Updated Edition

Carl Scriven
James Stevens

POINT LOMA NAZARENE COLLEGE
210013
WITHDRAWN
RYAN LIBRARY

VAN NOSTRAND REINHOLD
New York

Copyright © 1989 by Van Nostrand Reinhold

Copyright © 1982 by John Wiley & Sons, Inc.

Copyright © 1980 Conceptual Design

Library of Congress Catalog Card Number 88-27916
ISBN 0-442-31864-2

All rights reserved. No part of this work covered by the copyright
hereon may be reproduced or used in any form or by any means—
graphic, electronic, or mechanical, including photocopying, record-
ing, taping, or information storage and retrieval systems—without
written permission of the publisher.

Printed in the United States of America

Van Nostrand Reinhold
115 Fifth Avenue
New York, New York 10003

Van Nostrand Reinhold International Company Limited
11 New Fetter Lane
London EC4P 4EE, England

Van Nostrand Reinhold
480 La Trobe Street
Melbourne, Victoria 3000, Australia

Macmillan of Canada
Division of Canada Publishing Corporation
164 Commander Boulevard
Agincourt, Ontario MIS 3C7, Canada

16 15 14 13 12 11 10 9 8 7 6 5 4 3 2 1

Library of Congress Cataloging-in-Publication Data

Scriven, Carl.
    Food equipment facts.

    Includes index.
    1. Food service—Equipment and supplies.
I. Stevens, James, 1932–   . II. Title.
TX 912.S37   1989   641.5'7'028   88-27916
ISBN 0-442-31864-2

To our wives

JOYCE SCRIVEN
WINNIE STEVENS

WHAT WE DO OFFER THAT'S DIFFERENT

F.E.F. Personal Assistance Service: If you find any item in the book that you would appreciate more information on, send your request with a self-addressed, stamped, legal size envelope enclosed to:

F.E.F.
9 Glenmore Road
Troy, New York 12180

The information you request will be promptly returned.

THE AUTHORS

Jim Stevens (V.P. Sales) and Carl Scriven (Designer) together have over 50 years of experience in the Food Service Industry.

LIST OF CHAPTERS

LIST OF ILLUSTRATIONS

ACKNOWLEDGMENTS

The authors sincerely appreciate the cooperation received from the many manufacturers of food service and related equipment whose prompt responses to our request for additional information were a great aid in compiling this book. We gratefully acknowledge the assistance from our co-workers and the manufacturers reps who gave so freely of their time when and wherever it was needed.

Special thanks to:

MRS. JOAN STEFANACCI GILLESPIE, Secretary
Food Equipment Facts

MR. LARRY HOFF, District Manager
Hobart Corp.

MR. MIKE SNEDEKAR, Manufacturer's Representative
Ralph A. Meyer Associates

MR. RAY McDONALD, Manufacturer's Representative

MR. MO HILWEH, Owner
Plattsburgh Supply
(for Continued Support)

and particularly to

DR. JEROME J. VALLEN, Dean of
College of Hotel Administration
University of Nevada, Las Vegas

for his valued friendship and support.

FOOD
EQUIPMENT
FACTS

Chapter One

RECEIVING AREAS

Due to space and budget limitations adequate receiving areas are often neglected. However, today's inflationary prices certainly stress the importance of checking weights received. Where adequate space simply cannot be provided, a mobile table with a scale, having the capacity to check the weights of bulk products purchased, may be rolled into position at the receiving door and be used elsewhere the rest of the time.

Some things to remember when planning receiving areas are:
1. Standard dock height is from 36" to 44".
2. If a truck dock is structurally impossible, mobile and built-in hydraulic lift docks are available. (See Fig. 1-2)
3. Minimum door size is 36" x 6'8". Larger doors are recommended where space permits.
4. Provide ample space for all mobile equipment required to efficiently move merchandise received to its proper storage area.
5. Pest control is always a problem at receiving doors. Self-closing doors, double doors and "Fly Chasing Fans" are invaluable.
6. In establishments where bread or roll consumption is high, as in convenience markets, sandwich shops, hospitals, etc. space for the plastic, stacking racks with dollies should be considered. These are usually supplied by the bakery. The plastic trays measure approximately 31" x 22½" x 6" high and will hold 12 loaves of bread, 8 dozen rolls or the equivalent in each. They may be easily stacked 6 to 8 high and rolled directly to the point of use.
7. A small desk, even if wall mounted, is very useful and it is usually an excellent location for the time clock. Even in the best planned restaurants and institutions a hand sink and water fountain are often overlooked. Both are very useful in receiving areas.
8. Receiving areas should be well lighted and weather protected. Clear vinyl strip curtains for weather protection are listed in Chapter 3.

Following are a few facts on receiving areas and equipment to assist you in selecting the proper items.

SPACE REQUIRED FOR RECEIVING AREAS

The following chart shows suggested sizes for receiving areas in varying establishments. It must be kept in mind that exact sizes will vary depending on frequency of deliveries and menu variations.

Most hospitals and many other large in-plant facilities share dock space with other departments. In such cases only efficient transporting equipment need be considered.

Fig. 1-1

RESTAURANTS

Meals Per Day	200/300	300/500	500/1000	1000/1400	1400/1600
Area in Sq. Ft.	50/60	60/90	90/130	130/160	160/190

HOSPITALS · NURSING HOMES · EXTENDED CARE FACILITIES

Number of Beds	Up to 50	50/100	100/200	200/400
Area in Sq. Ft.	50	50/80	80/130	130/175

SCHOOLS

Meals Per Day	200/300	300/500	500/700	700/900	900/1000
Area in Sq. Ft.	30/40	40/60	60/75	75/90	90/100

IN-PLANT CAFETERIAS AND FOOD FACILITIES

Meals Per Day	200/400	400/800	800/1200	1200/1500
Area in Sq. Ft.	75/80	85/115	115/155	155/200

Hydraulic lift docks, mentioned above, are vertically rising platforms that provide a level surface onto which or over which loads can be transferred at any height between ground level and 58" above ground. They are designed to facilitate the loading and unloading of trucks at the dock. They have self-contained power units with controls. Hydraulic plungers lift or lower the platform in a level position employing scissor action supports.

Fig. 1-2

TYPICAL HYDRAULIC LIFT DOCKS

Type	Platform Size	Capacity	Lift Height	Lift Speed	HP	Wheels
Portable	6' x 6'	4,000 lb.	58"	8 FPM	1½	4" Dia.

STATIONARY DOCKS

Class	Platform Size	Capacity	Lift Speed	HP	Lowered Height
Light Duty	6' x 8'	5,000 lbs.	12 FPM	5	10"
Medium Duty	6' x 8' to 8' x 11'	5,000 lbs. to 6,000 lbs.	12 FPM	5	10"
Average Duty	6' x 8' to 8' x 10'	7,000 lbs. to 8,500 lbs.	8 FPM	5	12"

(Continued)

STATIONARY DOCKS (Cont.)					
Class	Platform Size	Capacity	Lift Speed	HP	Lowered Height
Heavy Duty	6' x 8' to 8' x 11'	10,000 lbs.	6 FPM	5	14''
Extra Heavy Duty	6' x 12' to 8' x 12'	18,000 lbs. to 20,000 lbs.	5 FPM	7½	18'' to 20''

There are also available Hydraulic Lift Docks designed to be installed flush with the pavement when in a lowered position.

Fig. 1-3

TYPICAL PLATFORM TRUCK SIZES

Platform Size	Wheel Dia.	Maximum Load
18'' x 30''	5'' to 6''	400 lbs.
24'' x 48''	6''	1000 lbs.
24'' x 48''	8''	1500 lbs.
27'' x 54''	6''	1000 lbs.
27'' x 54''	8''	1500 lbs.
30'' x 60''	6''	1000 lbs.
30'' x 60''	8''	1500 lbs.

STEEL PALLETS

Listed only are some standard sizes and the load limit of common steel pallets. Many other materials and systems are available.

Pallet sizes are 36'' x 48'', 40'' x 48'', 42'' x 42'', 42'' x 48'' and 48'' x 48''. All are 4'' high with a load limit of 10,000 lbs. They can be reversible or nonreversible and matching shelving and pallet jacks or lifts are available.

Also available for large commissary operations, is the Robotic Palletizer for cases, cans and trays of over 100 pounds or less. A built-in micro processor will accept and memorize the shortest distance, pick up, and placement points to complete loads of same size product. Back up cassette can store work patterns. Requires 6½ x 7' of floor space including pallets. Power consumption 1.5 KW.

HAND TRUCKS

Hand trucks are available in many styles and capacities. The average overall height is 49''. Light-duty hand trucks are available with 6'', 8'' and 10'' wheels with a load limit of 400 lbs. Heavy-duty

Standard options include remote indicator, metric switch, short or tall columns, casters.

NEW L.E.D. SCALES
with digital readout

These L.E.D. (light emitting diode) scales are the latest in electronic weighing devices and are becoming available in many models and sizes. Some typical models are described below.

Fig. 1-8

Maximum Capacity	Space Required	No.	Features
9.99 lbs.	12" x 12"	1	Readout mounted behind and above unit. Angled up for easy visibility. 6' grounded cord and plug.
9.99 lbs.	12" x 12"	2	Same as No. 1 but powered by rechargeable batteries for use in remote areas. Charge life 8 hrs. Scale may be used while batteries are being charged.
9.99 lbs.	7½" x 9"	3	Angled readout built into front of base. 6' grounded cord and plug.
50.00 lbs.	7½" x 9"	4	Same as No. 3 above.
50.00 lbs.	11" x 16-3/8"	5	Same as No. 1 above.
9.99 lbs.	7" x 7"	6	Remote readout module connects to base with 7' cable. Readout module is 7-1/8" x 5-3/8" x 2-5/8" high
75.00 lbs.	11" x 11"	7	Same as No. 6 above.

All units have automatic tare buttons. All are accurate to nearest one-hundredth of a pound.

Information on other or larger scales not available at this time.

Chapter Two

DRY STORAGE

Using valuable space properly is like putting money in the bank. The information in this chapter will help you achieve maximum storage capacity for your particular food service operation. Compute your specific needs which depend on variables, such as menu items, number of meals served and frequency of deliveries. Then use the following charts which show standard sizes matched with some product sizes.

AVERAGE SPACE REQUIRED FOR DRY STORAGE IN VARIOUS ESTABLISHMENTS

Fig. 2-1

SCHOOL LUNCH PROGRAMS					
Meals Served	200	400	600	800	1000
Square Ft. Required	150/250	250/350	350/450	450/550	550/650
HOSPITAL FOOD SERVICE					
No. of Beds	50	100	200	400	
Square Ft. Required	150/225	250/375	400/600	700/900	
EMPLOYEE FEEDING					
Meals Served	400	800	1200	1500	
Square Ft. Required	350/450	550/650	700/850	950/1050	
RESTAURANTS & CLUBS					
Meals Per Day	100-200	200-350	350-500	500-1000	
Square Ft. Required	120/200	200/250	250/400	300/650	

This chart is intended as a guide only as every food service establishment has its own individual requirements.

HELPFUL HINTS

Properly planned dry storage areas should be well ventilated, well lighted, have flexibility in shelving areas and wherever possible have floor drains and a washdown hose. When planning new storage rooms think in terms of rows of shelving with adequate aisles between. For example: a row of wall shelving, an aisle, another row of shelving (single or back to back), another aisle and a row of shelving along the opposite wall. Too often adding 3 or 4 feet to the width of a room accomplishes nothing. Be sure to place doors at aisles. A door in the corner of any room destroys valuable wall space.

TYPICAL SHELVING SIZES

Fig. 2-2

SHELF WIDTH	LENGTHS AVAILABLE
12" or 14"	24" - 30" - 36" - 42" - 48" - 60"
18" - 21" or 24"	24" - 30" - 36" - 42" - 48" - 60" - 72"

The above units are manufactured as flat or louvered metal shelves and open welded wire shelves. The open wire shelving is recommended where ventilation is important.

All are available in aluminum, galvanized, coated galvanized and stainless steel. Stainless steel is of course the ultimate finish for both wet and dry storage and is accepted by U.S.D.A. for direct food contact. Less toxic, is zinc plated shelving coated with non toxic epoxy. This shelving is suitable for wet storage such as walk-in coolers. Uncoated zinc plated shelving should be used for dry storage only. Various manufacturers have different trade names for the plating and coating materials they use. Be sure the material you select is suited to your needs.

The average shelf load limit is 1,000 lbs.

UPRIGHT SUPPORTS FOR SHELVING

Fig. 2-3

Widths	Heights Available
12"	26"
14"	31-32"
18"	36-37"
21"	53½"
24"	64", 75" or 86"

NOTE: Most shelving units are designed so that shelving in straight runs may be supported by common uprights, and may have corner brackets attached to the side of end shelves to make right angle turns without an additional upright. These features cut costs appreciably. See Page 13 - Planning Guide.

SOME AVAILABLE OPTIONAL EXTRAS FOR BASIC SHELVING:

Back Ledges	Label Strips	18 x 26 Pan Holders
Corner Braces	Sloping Shelves	Short Legs for Dunnage
Wheels	Shelf Dividers	Racks, 6"-8" & 10" above
Dollies	Pan Holders	Floor
Wall Mount Supports	Covers	Wine Shelves

SPACE SAVING TRACK STYLE SHELVING

Front and rear tracks mounted between two end units allow units in between to glide easily in either direction providing an access aisle where you want it.

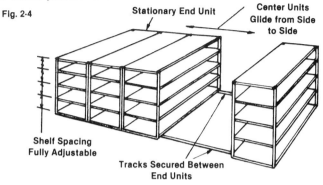

Fig. 2-4

Stationary End Unit

Center Units Glide from Side to Side

Shelf Spacing Fully Adjustable

Tracks Secured Between End Units

STANDARD SHELF UNIT SIZES
Widths: 20", 24"
Lengths: 36", 42", 48", 54"
Load Rating: 1,500 lbs. Per Unit

Heights are variable to suit your needs. The use of these units can increase storage capacity up to 40% or more depending on the number of units used.

Also available in top track sizes, the end units are stationary. Track systems run from six to twenty one feet in length. Shelf widths are usually 12, 18, 21, and 24 inches. Wider sizes becoming available soon.

CAN RACKS - MOBILE OR STATIONARY

These new style can holders provide for cans laying on sides to roll forward as needed. Easily loaded from rear; can be loaded from front. Loading from the rear provides automatic stock turnover first in - first out.

TYPICAL SIZES

Wide	Deep	High	Capacity
27"	38"	83"	30 Ctns. No. 10 Cans (180 Cans)
27"	38"	83"	21 Ctns. No. 10 Cans (126 Cans) + 8 Ctns. No. 5 Cans (96 Cans)
27"	38"	83"	28 Ctns. No. 5 Cans (336 Cans)
27"	38"	41"	12 Ctns. No. 10 Cans (72 Cans)

This unit available with work top for mounting a can opener and with casters so it may be rolled from store room to point of use.

Available also is a "roll forward" type rack which will store 5 cases (30) No. 10 cans and may be fitted to your existing shelving. These units load from the front at top, the cans roll downward and are removed from the bottom. This method of storing makes better use of shelf space and insures inventory turnover.

The unit is approximately 21" wide x 18¼" high x 40" long.

SPECIAL PURPOSE WIRE SHELVING
COMPONENTS AVAILABLE

MOBILE WORK STATIONS
LAUNDRY CARTS - top or side load
UTILITY CARTS
TRAY OR BUS BOX CARTS - with angle ledge glides
FULLY ENCLOSED CARTS - with sliding and locking doors
TRUCK AND VAN INTERIORS - with anchoring clips

Using standard components the above specialty units can be assembled. Various style wheels, brakes and finishes allow you to design your own vehicle.

TYPICAL MOBILE INGREDIENT BINS
FOR DRY STORAGE

Fig. 2-5

SIZES			Capacities			
Width	Depth	Height	Cu. Ft.	Gals.	Lbs. Sugar	Lbs. Flour
12" x 29" x 28"			3.4	26	175	125
21" x 23" x 28"			3.9	34	195	140
15" x 29" x 28"			4.4	34½	220	155
21" x 23" x 23"			5.1	43	260	185
18" x 29" x 28"			5.7	44	285	205

Many sizes and styles of ingredient bins are available in either plastics or metal and can be had with sliding or hinged covers.

The above chart can help you select one with the capacity you require.

Clear plastic, see through covers are available for many models.

PALLETS

Listed only are some standard sizes and the load limit of common steel pallets. Many other materials and systems are available.

Pallet sizes are 36" x 48", 40" x 48", 42" x 42", 42" x 48" and 48" x 48". All are 4" high with a load limit of 10,000 lbs. They can be reversible or nonreversible and matching shelving and pallet jacks or lifts are available.

STANDARD SIZES OF STORAGE ITEMS

The following charts show dimensions and capacities of many items commonly stored. Used in conjunction with the shelving charts these will help you attain maximum use of your dry storage area.

Fig. 2-6

STANDARD CANS				
Number	Dia.	Ht.	Capacity	4 Oz. Portions
2	3½''	5''	18 oz.	4½
2½	4''	5''	26 oz.	6½
3	4¼''	7½''	46 oz.	11½
10	6¼''	7½''	96 oz.	24

Fig. 2-7

APPROX. CAN CARTON SIZES		
Can	Per Carton	Carton Size
#2	24	14'' x 10'' x 9¼''
#2½	24	17'' x 12'' x 10¼''
#3	12	17½'' x 13½'' x 7¾''
#10	6	19'' x 12¾'' x 7¼''

CHINA AND GLASSWARE CARTON SIZES

To aid you in planning storage shelf space Fig. 2-8 shows sizes of the most commonly used china and glassware.

Fig. 2-8

Item	Carton Size
6¼'' Plates	9½'' x 13'' x 6¾'' High
9'' Plates	9½'' x 13½'' x 6¾'' High
Cups	13'' x 16'' x 9½'' High
Saucers	10½'' x 12¾'' x 6¾'' High
Bowls	9½'' x 16'' x 10'' High
Monkey Dishes	9¼'' x 10¼'' x 5½'' High
8 oz. Bulge Glasses	16½'' x 16¾'' x 8½'' High
8 oz. Stemware	19'' x 18½'' x 6¼'' High

— NOTES —

Chapter Three

REFRIGERATED
STORAGE

In this chapter we examine "back of the house" refrigeration such as walk-ins and kitchen refrigerators and freezers. The facts shown and information given will aid prospective buyers and students in selecting, by size, refrigeration requirements matched to menu items and frequency of deliveries. Out front, point of service refrigeration including such items as pastry and salad display cases will be covered in Chapter 7 (Serving, Holding and Transporting).

The options and variations available for refrigerators, freezers and walk-in units are numerous. It will pay to study them carefully. The initial costs may have a rapid pay back in energy savings and improved service.

A word of warning regarding freezers: They are not blast freezing units and overloading with unfrozen products will cause problems.

WALK-IN COOLERS AND FREEZERS

With no intent to be facetious the authors of Food Equipment Facts would like to state that in order to absolutely and scientifically size a walk-in cooler or freezer for any given establishment it would be necessary to know the exact menu to be served with any forseeable changes itemized. To know the number and frequencies of deliveries of all items. To have accurate predictions of the ebb and flow of patrons which would necessitate an equally accurate prediction of the future economic status of the community as well as changing weather conditions. If all this information can be assembled and the patrons arrive in the predicted numbers and eat the precise amounts of the specified menu items, your walk-in cooler can be scientifically sized, providing, of course, that the chef doesn't quit or come up with some fancy ideas of his own.

Don't panic dear reader, following are a number of charts and facts to aid you in making at least an intelligent, if not scientific selection of refrigerated equipment. May we remind you of our offer to help you locate full service equipment representatives or consultants covering your area. A stamped, self addressed envelope mailed with your specific request is all that is needed.

WALK-IN COOLER/FREEZER COMPONENTS

Nearly all modular walk-ins have the same general construction and assembly methods as well as the same optional variations. The individual panels which make up the units are usually 4" thick. The ain difference is in the height and width of the panels and corner pieces. Some manufacturers use modules of even 1'-0" divisions. When assembled their coolers could measure 8'-0" x 12'-0". Another manufacturer's unit of comparable size might measure 7'-8" x 11'-6" or 7'-9" x 11'-7" etc. It is important to consider these variations when planning shelving for the walk-ins. Standard heights of common walk-ins average 7'-6", 8'-6" and 10'-6". Modular paneling and interior support systems are available for constructing huge two story refrigerated warehouses. These require a considerable amount of engineering and will not be discussed in this book.

There are available many standard options for walk-in refrigeration units. They are listed below and there careful consideration, coupled with the charts which follow will aid in selecting the proper units for your use.

WALK-IN REFRIGERATOR OPTIONS

Before discussing options and their advantages let us remind you of our statement regarding planning dry storage areas. Plan your rows of shelving with the aisle space you require keeping in mind that simply adding 2 or 3 feet more width to the walk-in box may accomplish nothing more than adding extra cost to the unit.

1. Walk-ins are available for either indoor or outdoor installations. Outdoor units require weather caps for the roof and rain hoods are available for the doors. The compressors may be self-contained and winterized if required. Don't forget the condensate drain line from the blower coils.
2. Indoor units are available in various finishes and with decorator color panels.
3. Walk-in coolers may set directly on an existing concrete or tile floor using screeds available for this purpose, thereby eliminating the step up at the door. This should not be attempted with freezers.
4. To recess the walk-in floor to be level with the outside floor or to carry a tile floor into the walk-in units all manufacturers have detailed drawings of suggested designs to aid your contractor.
5. Where the walk-in floor is to set on an existing floor, interior floor panels with built-in ramps are available for coolers (not to be used in freezers) and outside ramps are available for either. Skid-proof treads are recommended.
6. Reinforced Floors — Diamond tread aluminum, etc. vary by manufacturer. Check with your supplier.
7. Pressure relief vents are available and strongly recommended especially in large freezer units. Warm air will fill the walk-in as the cold air runs out during stocking-up periods. Then when the door is closed the air contracts as it cools building up a partial vacuum inside making it very difficult to open the door. The

author remembers well a college installation where the chef used a crowbar to yank open the freezer door and collapsed the roof of the unit. We won't mention who installed the unit.

8. Thermometers, usually built into door panels, are available and called for by health departments in some areas.

9. Audio and visual alarm systems are available for both coolers and freezers.

10. About Doors — Standard door panels which usually contain the thermometer, the vapor proof light and switch and the door heater cables are available with 24", 30" and 34" wide doors hinged to right or left. Self-closing hinges are available. Door pulls are available with cylinder locks or pad lock holes. Inside safety releases are standard. Foot treadle openers may be ordered. Glass view ports with triple thick glass, heated for freezers may be installed. Kick plates and bumper strips may be attached. Track ports above the door opening are available where overhead trolley systems are used.

Reach-in doors, either one above the other or one door at top are available in glass or solid, hinged either side or sliding.

Full height glass display doors with built-in adjustable shelving, vertical fluorescent lighting and heater cables to prevent condensation are available either hinged or sliding. These units may be installed adjacent to each other for the full length of the cooler or freezer.

Sliding doors, either manual or powered are available in various widths for use where hinged doors are impractical or where fork lift trucks are used. They may be right or left sliding or bi-parting.

11. Various options are available for the refrigeration systems. They may be self-contained with the compressor mounted on top of the unit. Saddle mounted with the condensing unit and the blower coils hung over a wall panel or self-contained remote systems have pre-charged snap-on refrigerant lines allowing the compressor to be located in any convenient spot within approximately 20 feet.

12. Plastic air curtains hung at door openings can cut down running time of the compressor and save money for you. These are detailed later in this chapter.

Before we move on let us remind you not to forget about the condensate drain lines from the blower coils. This can be a real headache on a union job. They must be trapped, then run to an indirect waste and a heater tape is required in the freezer. Floor drains are not permissible inside of walk-in boxes. Secondly, be sure of your voltage, phase and horsepower in that they are compatible with your power supply. Last but by no means least, check your warranty.

NOTE: All of the above options for walk-in units may not be available from any single manufacturer.

SOME SPECIALIZED WALK-INS

A somewhat specialized walk-in unit is produced with limited options but with some unique features. The most important feature is that the entire refrigeration unit is built into one 2'-0" x 2'-0" corner panel, forming a triangle on the inside. The unit is completely factory sized and assembled and requires only one electrical connection. The panels are in even 1'-0" modules and are only 2½" thick. The metal floor is backed with ¼" plywood. The units are available with or without the floor panels. The sizes available are shown in Fig. 3-1.

Fig. 3-1

OVERALL SIZE W/FLOOR			COMPRESSOR RATING	
Height	Width	Depth	Cooler	Freezer
7'-5½"	6'	8'	¾ HP	1½ HP
7'-5½"	8'	8'	¾ HP	1½ HP
7'-5½"	8'	10'	1 HP	2 HP
7'-5½"	6'	10'	¾ HP	1½ HP
7'-5½"	10'	10'	1 HP	2 HP
7'-5½"	6'	12'	1 HP	2 HP
7'-5½"	8'	12'	1 HP	2 HP

One manufacturer produces sectional wood panel units sheathed with ¾" fir. A unit ideally suited to palletized warehousing has one front panel 14'-8" wide 9'-6" high with two biparting folding aluminum clad doors which open full width. Some typical sizes and capacities are shown in Fig. 3-2. Others available.

Units are well suited to beverage, dairy or general utility storage.

Fig. 3-2

Width	Depth	½ BARREL CAPACITIES			Cases (66)	Refr. Req'd.
		Squat (4 high)	Tall (3 high)	Corded		
14'-8"	16'-6"	312	240	192	1056	2 HP
14'-8"	20'-6"	378	288	240	1320	3 HP
14'-8"	24'-6"	440	336	288	1584	3 HP
14'-8"	28'-6"	568	384	336	1848	3 HP

For those who may be searching this chapter for a beer cooler, the manufacturers of the above mentioned wood clad boxes produce a unique unit where one side is stepped out to form a back bar with top and a drainer plate, the upper portion is fitted with a direct draw, simulated barrel head and glass reach-in doors may be installed on the other side for wine display. Behind the back-bar wall is a full height walk-in cooler. From the inside a row of barrels may be stored under the protruding back-bar and tapped for direct draw. This unit may be constructed to your dimensional requirements.

Working down from large walk-ins to standard reach-in refrigerators and freezers we come to step-in units. These vary in size by manufacturer. One measuring 62" wide x 49" deep x 75½" high plus approximately 18" with compressor top mounted has 79 cu.ft. of storage space. As a cooler it is available with either ⅓ or ½ HP compressor. As a freezer either a ¾ or 1 HP compressor is available. The 1 HP would be required for ice cream storage. Capacities are 60 milk cases or 24 egg cases. As a freezer it will hold 140 frozen food cases measuring 8" x 3" x 13" or 560 gallons of ice cream.

ESTIMATING SPACE REQUIREMENTS

Hundreds of charts, figures and facts have been printed in many different books. Those relating to primary schools, hospitals, nursing homes, military installations and so on, where the variables are kept to a minimum, can be and are often very accurate. For the average independent owner who is almost always faced with limited budgets and space it can be quite a dilemma. One statement which may be very helpful is that in the years that the authors have worked together they have found that in the average restaurant having 100 to 150 seats with normal buying practices and average deliveries a walk-in cooler 7'-8" wide x 11'-6" deep x 7'-6" high with a freezer section approximately 5'-9" deep added to it has proven very satisfactory.

A general rule of thumb for estimating walk-in refrigeration is to allow ½ cubic foot of usable space per meal served. Small walk-ins with only one door and a single aisle can have from 50% to 60% of usable space. Larger walk-ins with multiple aisles and doors can drop to from 35% to 45% usable space.

Use the charts for standard shelving in Chapter 2, consider dunnage racks, mobile bins, and rolling angle ledge banquet carts, then use the following information to help in your selection of walk-in units.

REFRIGERATED STORAGE FOR VARIOUS OPERATIONS
(Expressed as Total Square Feet)

Fig. 3-3

In Plant Feeding	Meals Per Day	400	800	1200	1600
	Sq. Ft. Required	75-120	115-135	140-175	170-210
Schools	Meals Per Day	200	400	500	1000
	Sq. Ft. Required	25-35	35-50	50-75	75-100
Central	No. of Beds	50	100	150-200	400
Hospitals	Sq. Ft. Required	40-50	80-100	200	400

RESTAURANT NEEDS BY TOTAL CUBIC FEET

Fig. 3-4

Average 3 Meal/Day	1 to 1½ Usable Cu. Ft. Per Person
Fine Dining - 1 Meal/Day	2 to 5 Usable Cu. Ft. Per Seat

(Note **usable** cu. ft. regarding walk-ins)

EXAMPLE

From the chart above a 150 seat fine dining restaurant using a figure of 3.5 cu.ft./seat could require 525 cu. ft. of refrigeration. This might break down as follows:

Walk-in using approx. inside dimensions of
7' high unit — 7' x 11' cooler + 7' x 5' freezer

total cu. ft. 784 - 40% usable space	313
2 Door Chef's refrigerator	47
1 Door Chef's freezer	17
2 Door undercounter refrigerator	15
Refrigerated open cold pan	10
Sandwich unit	12
Waitress pantry refrigeration	47
Dessert display refrigerator	47
TOTAL CUBIC FEET	508

The above chart was compiled as a brainstorming guide only and should not be considered to be an absolute requirement list for any particular operation. It is however typical of any average restaurant, take away the cold pan and add an ice cream cabinet, etc. One thing to note is that with using the comparatively low figure of 40% the usable walk-in storage space is approximately 3/5 of the total refrigeration required.

Another rule of thumb that may help is that on the average 45 lbs. of solid foods will equal 1 cubic foot.

POUNDS OF FOOD PER SHELF
(By width stored 12" high)

12" wide: 45 lbs./ft. — 14" wide: 52 lbs./ft. — 18" wide: 67 lbs./ft. — 21" wide: 79 lbs./ft. — 24" wide: 90 lbs./ft.

PER CENT OF SPACE REQUIRED BY PRODUCT

Meats	20/25%	Dairy Products	20/25%
Fruit & Vegetables	30/35%	Salads & Desserts	10/15%

20

TYPICAL VOLUME CONSUMED BY GROUP

Meat or Poultry................010 to .030 Cu. Ft. Per Meal
Dairy Products.................007 to .015 Cu. Ft. Per Meal
Vegetables & Fruit............020 to .040 Cu. Ft. Per Meal

(Low figure would be 1 meal service as school lunch — High figure
would represent typical full service restaurant.)

The following chart was compiled from one popular manufacturer's catalog. Other manufacturers standard modules will vary only slightly. Since the combinations of sizes are made nearly infinite by varying widths and heights of wall, door and corner panels only a limited typical number are shown and only two heights are given. Many others are available.

Fig. 3-5   **TYPICAL WALK-IN SIZES SHOWING SQ. FT., CU. FT.
AND REFRIGERATION REQUIREMENTS**

WALK-IN UNIT SIZE	SQ. FT. INTERIOR FLOOR	CUBIC FEET INTERIOR OF WALK-IN		REFRIGERATION REQUIRED	
		7'-6" High	8'-6" High	Cooler Either Hgt.	Freezer Either Hgt.
5'-9" x 4'-9"	20.9	146.3	167.2	½ HP	1 HP
5'-9" 7'8"	35.7	259.9	285.6	½ HP	1 HP
5-9" x 9'7"	45.4	317.8	363.2	¾ HP	1½ HP
5'-9" x 12'-5½"	60.1	420.7	480.8	1 HP	1½ HP
5'-9" x 14'-4½"	70.8	495.6	566.4	1 HP	2 HP
5'-9" x 17'-3"	84.1	588.7	672.8	1½ HP	2 HP
5'-9" x 20'-1½"	98.9	692.3	791.2	1½ HP	2 HP
6'-8½" x 8'-7½"	47.4	331.8	379.2	¾ HP	1½ HP
6'-8½" x 11'-6"	64.2	449.4	513.6	1 HP	1½ HP
6-8½" x 14'-4½"	82.2	575.4	657.6	1½ HP	2 HP
6-8½" x 18'-2½"	105.6	739.2	844.8	1½ HP	2 HP
7'-8" x 7'-8"	49.0	340.2	392.1	¾ HP	1½ HP
7'-8" x 11'-6"	75.6	529.2	604.8	1 HP	2 HP
7'-8" x 18'-2½"	122.5	857.5	980.1	2 HP	2 HP
7'-8" x 20'-1½"	138.8	971.6	1110.4	2 HP	3 HP
8'-7½" x 11'-6"	86.4	604.8	691.2	1½ HP	2 HP
8'-7½" x 16'-3½"	123.2	862.4	985.6	2 HP	2 HP
8'-7½" x 19'-2"	146.4	1024.8	1171.2	2 HP	3 HP
9'-7" x 11'-6"	98.1	686.7	784.8	1½ HP	2 HP

(Continued)

Fig. 3-5

TYPICAL WALK-IN SIZES SHOWING SQ. FT., CU. FT. AND REFRIGERATION REQUIREMENTS

WALK-IN UNIT SIZE	SQ. FT. INTERIOR FLOOR	CUBIC FEET INTERIOR OF WALK-IN		REFRIGERATION REQUIRED	
		7'-6" High	8'-6" High	Cooler Either Hgt.	Freezer Either Hgt.
9'-7" x 15'-4"	131.4	919.8	1051.2	2 HP	2 HP
9'-7" x 18'-2½"	157.5	1102.5	1260.2	2 HP	3 HP
10'-6½" x 12'-5½"	117.2	820.4	937.6	1½ HP	2 HP
10'-6½" x 16'-3½"	158.1	1106.7	1264.8	2 HP	3 HP
10'-6½" x 20'-1½"	196.4	1379.8	1671.2	2 HP	3 HP
11'-6" x 13'-5"	140.8	985.6	1126.4	1½ HP	2 HP
11'-6" x 18'-2½"	194.7	1362.9	1557.6	2 HP	3 HP
12'-5½" x 13'-5"	145.2	1016.4	1161.6	1½ HP	2 HP
12'-5½" x 16'-3½"	182.4	1276.8	1459.2	2 HP	3 HP
12'-5½" x 20'-1½"	230.4	1612.8	1843.2	2 HP	3 HP

Use Fig. 3-6 and Fig. 3-7 to help in determining shelf spacing, width and height.

Fig. 3-6

SIZE OF COMMON REFRIGERATOR ITEMS

Item	Package	Approx. Capacity	Height	Width or Dia.	Length
Butter	Box	64 lb.	12"	12"	14"
Cheese	Wheel	20-23 lb.	7½"	13½"	
Eggs	Case	45 lb.	13"	12"	26"
Milk	Can	10 gal.	25"	13½"	
	Case	24½ pt.	10½"	13"	13"
	Case	24½ pt.	7"	13"	19"
Margarine	Box	60 lb.	10"	14"	17½"
Meat, portioned	Tray	40 lb.	3"	18"	26"
Cuts	Box	40 lb.	6"	18"	28"
Cuts	Box	50 lb.	10"	10"	28"
Apples	Box	35-40	10½"	11½"	18"
	Carton	40-45 lb.	12"	12½"	20"
Berries	Crate	36 lb.	11"	11"	22"
Cherries, Grapes	Lug	25-30 lb.	6"	13½"	16"
Citrus	Crate	65-80 lb.	12"	12"	26"
	Carton	40-65 lb.	11"	11½"	17"

Fig. 3-7

SIZES AND SPACE REQUIRED FOR SOME
FROZEN FOOD ITEMS

| Item | BOXES OR CARTONS | | No. of Units which can be stored per cu.ft. |
	Capacity	Package Size	
Vegetables	2½ lb.	9-5/8" x 5-3/8" x 2½"	13
French Fries	30 lb.	18" x 11½" x 10-1/8"	.83
Fish Sticks	6 lb.	10-1/8" x 8-1/8" x 2¾"	7
Lobster Tails	5 lb.	15" x 7¼" x 3-3/8"	4
Trout	5 lb.	13" x 8¼" x 2¾"	6
Shrimp	5 lb.	11-5/8" x 6¼" x 2¾"	8
Chicken Parts	10 lb.	18¼" x 10¾" x 2¾"	3
Ground Beef	50 lb.	20¾" x 15¾" x5¼"	1
Butter	32 lb.	11" x 11" x 11"	1
Cheese	30 lb.	12" x 12" x 8½"	1.3
Ice Cream Carton	½ gal.	7" x 4¾" x 3½"	15
Ice Cream Round	2½ gal.	9½" Dia. x 10"	1
Fruit	30 lb.	10" Dia. x 13"	1
Fruit	#10 can	6-1/8" Dia. x 7"	10
Fruit	#5 can	4¼" Dia. x 7"	13
Orange Juice	2½ lb.	4-1/8" Dia. x 5½"	19
Concentrated	12 oz.	2¾" Dia. x 5"	49
Concentrated	32 oz.	4" Dia. x 5-5/8"	19

CLEAR HEAVY VINYL, OVERLAPPING DOOR STRIPS

Hung inside of walk-in cooler doors they form an excellent barrier to keep the cold air in. They have many other energy saving applications. Heavier nylon reinforced, double overlapping units are available for outdoor installations such as receiving dock doors. Curtain should be sized 2" over door size on each side and at top wherever possible.

SOME STANDARD SIZES

34"W x 80"H	53"W x 84"H	66"W x 84"H	79"W x 84"H
34"W x 84"H	53"W x 96"H	66"W x 96"H	79"W x 96"H
40"W x 80"H	53"W x 108"H	66"W x 108"H	79"W x 108"H
40"W x 84"H	53"W x 120"H	66"W x 120"H	79"W x 120"H
40"W x 96"H	60"W x 84"H	73"W x 84"H	86"W x 84"H
40"W x 108"H	60"W x 96"H	73"W x 96"H	86"W x 96"H
40"W x 120"H	60"W x 108"H	73"W x 108"H	86"W x 108"H
47"W x 84"H	60"W x 120"H	73"W x 120"H	86"W x 120"H
47"W x 96"H			92"W x 84"H
47"W x 108"H			92"W x 96"H
47"W x 120"H			92"W x 108"H
			92"W x 120"H

WRAP AROUND HEAT TAPES

Protection to 50° Below Zero
120 Volt

Fig. 3-11

Standard Lengths	Watts
6 ft.	30 Watts
9 ft.	45 Watts
13 ft.	65 Watts
18 ft.	90 Watts
24 ft.	120 Watts
45 ft.	225 Watts
60 ft.	300 Watts
100 ft.	800 Watts

Needed for walk in freezer evaporator drain lines.

SOME STANDARD BLAST FREEZER SIZES

Fig. 3-12

CAPACITIES OF BLAST FREEZERS 10° to 15°			
Size	Cu. Ft.	Ice Cream Storage	Frozen Food Storage
8' W x 8' L x 8½' H	318	1400 gals.	270 cases
8' W x 10' L x 8½' H	416	1800 gals.	400 cases
8' W x 12' L x 8½' H	514	2000 gals.	480 cases
8' W x 14' L x 8½' H	612	2500 gals.	570 cases
8' W x 16' L x 8½' H	710	2900 gals.	680 cases
8' W x 20' L x 8½' H	906	3700 gals.	870 cases
8' W x 22' L x 8½' H	1004	4100 gals.	920 cases
8' W x 26' L x 8½' H	1200	4800 gals.	1150 cases
8' W x 28' L x 8½' H	1298	5000 gals.	1300 cases

Ice Cream: Figured in rectangular ½ gallon packages.
Frozen Food Case Size: 12" W x 17" L x 5" H.
All storage capacity for blast freezers allows for working aisles and air space over stored product.

REMOTE REFRIGERATION

Nearly all refrigeration units may be ordered for remote compressor installations. The advantages should be seriously considered.

1. Remoting to a cool, dust-free area will increase the life of the compressor.
2. It can increase the cubic capacity of the refrigeration unit, especially in under counter units where space is a premium.
3. It eliminates objectionable running noises.
4. The units may be easily serviced or switched leaving working aisles free during a rush period.

5. It could be advantageous to have one local refrigeration company supply all of your units.
6. Systems are available with combined heating and cooling devices built into an enclosed compressor rack that supply controlled temperature at which the compressors operate most efficiently and in turn reduce energy cost and increase compressor life. These units are described in Chapter 14.

REACH-IN REFRIGERATORS AND FREEZERS

Before selecting a refrigerator or for that matter, any piece of equipment, study all of the available options and consider how they may benefit you. Listed below is a check list of options for refrigerators and where applicable, for freezers.

1. Single door units may have full doors or half doors, either glass or solid. Other than the obvious advantage of glass doors for display refrigerators they can save a lot of time in searching for items with the door open where the unit may be used by different operators, waitresses, etc. Half doors lose comparatively little in cubic content and can save in refrigeration loss as opposed to frequent opening of full doors.

   Multiple door refrigerators, in addition to the above may have sliding doors. These are advantageous where aisle space is limited but only one person can use a two door unit at one time.

   Doors may be either right or left hand hinged. Be sure you order the best one to suit your purpose.
2. Refrigerator/freezer combinations are available in many configurations. Single width units may be over-under models with the freezer either above or below the refrigerator. Multiple door boxes are available with thermostatically controlled hot sections having indicator lights and heat adjustment up to 200°. These may be ordered in any combination up to 3 sections wide; i.e., refr./freezer, refr./hot, hot/refr./freezer, etc. In order of right to left sequence any arrangement is available.

   Combination refrigerator/freezers may be operated from one compressor or have two, either self contained or remote of course.
3. Pass-through units have doors front and back, particularly suited to through wall service.
4. Roll-in or roll-through units for angle ledge carts. Especially useful for banquet set-up, resorts, etc.
5. Finished backs may be placed on refrigerated units to be installed in open spaces.
6. Refrigerated drawers are very convenient when installed in under-counter or work top refrigerators. Not suited to freezers. A considerable amount of storage space is lost.

7. Fish storage cabinets (handy at broiling stations) have drawers with drain lines which permits icing the stored fillets. Detailed later in this chapter.
8. Check the available interior and exterior finishes your suppliers has to offer, i.e., plastic, stainless steel, aluminum, enamel, decorator color panels, etc.
9. Some units have exterior thermometers as standard, others as optional.
10. Interior lights are not always standard.
11. Newer models have energy saving condensate evaporators and door defoggers which employ internal heat from the condensing coils.
12. Casters are a convenient option to make housekeeping easy.
13. In locations where height may be a problem units are available with the compressor mounted in the bottom using the lower portion of one section leaving approximately a 2/3 sized door in that section. The average overall height of these is 74".

UPRIGHT REACH-IN UNITS

Fig. 3-13

TYPICAL SIZES BY FULL DOORS						
Doors	Cu. Ft.	Height	Width	Depth	High Temp.	Low Temp.
1	22	78"-83"	28"	32"	¼ HP	½ HP
2	50	78"-83"	56"	32"	⅓ HP	¾ HP
3	70-80	78"-83"	84"	32"	½ HP	1 HP
4	100	78"	113"	32½"	¾ HP	(2) ¾ HP

(Sizes are average only. Vary by manufacturer.)

HELPFUL HINTS

A three or four door refrigerator is a very large piece of equipment which will stubbornly resist making a sharp turn in a narrow hallway, will often balk at passing through a normal door opening and can hardly ever be forced to ascend average stairways. Be sure the one you order will enter gracefully.

PAN SLIDES

Pan slide refrigerator storage systems are an option worthy of special attention. Details and dimensions vary by manufacturer. Some have pan slide cages which rest on standard shelving. Others are designed to hold either 18" x 26" pans or 12" x 20" or both when fitted with the proper angle slides.

Below is a check list for sizing pans and portions:

1. Determine plate, bowl or glass size.
2. How many fit on an 18" x 26" pan.
3. Measure height of product on pan to determine spacing.
4. Total the number of portions required.
5. Check the number of trays, by centers to door openings from charts below.
6. Be sure to use the wider angle glides when using 12" x 20" or other pans or trays.

TYPICAL PAN HOLDING CAPACITIES PER DOOR OPENING
(Using 18" x 26" pans 1" deep)

Fig. 3-14

Slide Centers	Half Doors	Full Doors
1"	27 Pans	57 pans
1½"	18 Pans	36 Pans
2"	13 Pans	28 Pans
2¼"	12 Pans	24 Pans
3"	9 Pans	19 Pans
4"	7 Pans	14 Pans
5"	5 Pans	11 Pans
6"	4 Pans	9 Pans

ROLL IN PROOFER–RETARDER

A unique two door proofer-retarder with a control system that allows manual operation of either "Proof" or "Retard" on demand. This unit can also be programmed by a 24 hour timer and time relay to automatically adjust from the humidity controlled cabinet to the air circulated refrigeration mode. Inside temperature is governed by an adjustable preset control. Maximum size rack usable is 27" wide, 29" deep and 72" high. This combination unit requires incoming water line, two drain lines and comes in various voltages.

AUXILIARY AIR COOLER
For Walk-in Boxes

Unit is 16" H x 48" L x 6" D. Bolts to interior wall of walk-in cooler with intake and exhaust ducts to outside atmosphere. In winter months whenever temperature drops below the thermostatic setting, the intake fan pulls the cold air in. A separate exhaust fan returns it to the ATMOSPHERE. Saves wear and running cost of compressors during cold weather months. Kit packaged, easy to install. Roof styles available, normal maximum run is 15 running feet from outside area.

TYPICAL CAPACITIES OF FOOD ITEMS ON 18" x 26" PANS

Fig. 3-15

Item	Size	Portions Per Pan	Slide Centers	No. of Pans Per 100 Portions
Milk	½ Pt.	40	4"	2½
Cole Slaw	Fruit Dish	21	3"	5
Salad	6" Bowl	11	3"	9
Pie	6-3/8" Plate	11	2"	9
Fruit Cup	Sherbet	40	4"	2½
Fruit Juice	5 oz. Glass	84	4"	1¼
Cream	1 oz. Cup	125	2"	1
Cantaloupe	7-3/8 Plate	8	3"	12½

FISH STORAGE REFRIGERATORS

These cabinets are available in single or double tiers. Each tier contains 4 drawers. The units are 26" deep x 83" high. The single unit is 28" wide. The double 52-1/8" wide. Remote models approximately 71" high. Total drawer capacity 4.5 cu. ft. for the single unit and 9.0 cu. ft. for the double. Compressors ¼ HP for the 4 drawer and ⅓ HP for the 8 drawer unit. Options are limited — dimensions vary by manufacturer. Units require an indirect waste line.

WORK TOP UNITS

These units, averaging 34½" high including legs, and are designed to fit under existing work tables. The tops being sheathed with metal in the same manner as the sides. They may also be ordered as complete units with tops of your choice in stainless steel, plastic or wood with or without back or end splashes. Standard options such as pan slides, right or left door swing, various finishes, remote refrigeration, casters, etc. may be included. All refrigeration units vary considerably in design and size; i.e., some manufacturers use as little as 12" of width for compressors while others occupy up to 24". These variances are most important when you are comparing bid prices and particularly when the unit must fit in a tight space. Figure 3-16 shows three popular sizes of self-contained units to assist in selection of one to fill your requirements.

Fig. 3-16

WORK TOP UNITS

Doors	Cu. Ft.	Width	Depth	Refr HP	Freezer HP
1	8.4	50"	33"	1/5	1/3
2	18.3	77 ¼ "	33"	1/4	1/3
3	28.2	105"	33"	1/3	1/2

FULL SIZE SANDWICH UNITS

The units described here are those that will accept full size pans (12" x 20") as these are most practical for in-kitchen work. Other, more common units with smaller pan capacities are covered in Chapter 7, Holding and Serving. Again, variations and options must be considered.

Fig. 3-17

SANDWICH UNITS

Doors	Cu. Ft.	12" x 20" Pans	H.P.	Width	Depth	Height To Top
1	10	3	1/4	46"	32-5/8"	34"
2	14	4	1/4	60"	32-5/8"	34"
3	18	5	1/4	74"	32-5/8"	34"

These units may have telescoping removable covers and cutting boards. The 12" x 20" openings may be fitted with adapters to hold round inserts for salad dressings. They will of course also accept any standard combinations of pans. See Chapter 8 for capacities.

PIZZA MAKE-UP TABLES

These also vary in dimension and design by manufacturer. The size of the compressor housing is usually the greatest variance. This will effect the cubic content. The units average 39" in overall height x 32" deep. Some have condiment shelves at the rear with the pans being inserted into cut-outs in the shelf and not refrigerated. The more desirable units have the pan insert elevated at the rear of the working top and the pans are refrigerated. Check with your supplier regarding the style, number and size of the pans.

Pizza tables are available with marble, plastic composition, stainless steel or wood tops. Three typical sizes are listed below to aid in your selection.

1. TRIPLE TEMPERATURE CABINETS. Convertible from $0°$ freezer to $28°$ chiller to $40°$ refrigerator.

2. RAPID COOL REFRIGERATOR. Convected air cools $104°$ degree foods rapidly through the danger zone for bacterial growth to $40°$. May be used as standard $38°$ refrigerator.

3. RAPID DEFROST. Alternating heated and refrigerated forced air bring food rapidly through defrosting. May also be used as a conventional refrigerator.

4. RAPID FREEZER. Two styles, one using air blast the other, nitrogen spray, can bring food temperature down to $-100°$ depending on style used. Either converts to $-5°$ freezer.

5. A single door unit is available for use where traffic is heavy and the door would normally be opened and closed frequently, i.e. waitress' stations. The door to this refrigerator may be lifted off at rush hours. A curtain of air blows across the opening keeping the cold air in and the hot air out.

6. DOUGH RETARDERS. High humidity refrigeration systems, usually feature oversize coils, to produce maximum temperataure conditions that retard the rising of doughs. Sizes for most applications are the same as standard reach ins and under counter refrigerators.

THE LITTLE FELLOWS

Let it not be said that we overlooked the little office refrigerator so necessary during conferences with visiting V.I.P.'s, in the event that one should feel the need for a refreshing glass of cool spring water.

There is available a wood grained vinyl finished model measuring only 23" wide x 34½" x 23" deep in which an unbelievable amount of mixers, snacks, juices, condiments, ice cubes and a selection of tall, thin, brown bottles may be stored. Ice cubes in the full width freezer drawer, the remainder on the two shelves below it or in the door rack. The cubic content is 6.5 and the little rascal even has a door frame to accept ¼" paneling to match your office decor. A visiting clergyman or your mother-in-law might not even notice it's there.

For those who for some unimaginable reason may require more ice, a cuber is available for the unit which will produce approximately 550 cubes per day with a storage bucket to hold 312 more. This only leaves 2.1 cu. ft. of storage space in the refrigerator, but what the heck — the good stuff is in another cabinet anyhow.

If you have noticed a trend toward longer conferences around the holiday season, a matching ice machine measuring only 14" x 14" x 24" high, that will produce another 550 cubes per day and store up to 300 more is available.

COUNTER TOP FREEZER

A new style counter top ice cream freezer is available that will hold up to 200 novelty items. Portable, this freezer features lift up or lift off lid. Size: 21" wide, 32" deep, 17" high.

PORTABLE TABLE TOP SANDWICH UNIT

A compact portable refrigerated sandwich unit that plugs in a standard outlet, will fit any counter and is ideal for a salad prep area. Also ideal for short term holding in fast food or take out operations. Featuring adjustable temperature controls, built in temperature indicator, this unit holds 6 ⅛ size pans and 2 ⅙ size pans. (See pan chart page for actual pan capacities.) Sizes are 53½" long, 12" deep and 11¼" high.

F.E.F. HUMOR

Quite a few years ago beer systems using recirculating ice water to chill the beer lines were new and also relatively expensive as compared to ice cooling or air shaft installations. Our firm did quite a bit of promotion for the system it carried. Being both new and expensive didn't make them easy to sell and any lead was promptly pursued.

A reply card from a mailing came in one morning with a request for information on the new beer system. Our top salesman was sent out on the lead. To everyone's joy and surprise, he came back a few hours later with a bonafide order for a complete system.

We were a lot more surprised when we discovered that he had gone to the wrong address.

HELPFUL HINTS

Nearly everyone understands that compressors for refrigeration units are sized by Horsepower ranging anywhere from 1/5 HP or smaller, all the way up to 3 HP or larger. They usually have a reasonably accurate conception of the capabilities of a 1/4 HP, a 1 HP, etc. but, just exactly why air-conditioning units are rated by tons is generally a complete mystery to them.

It may surprise you to know that the American Refrigeration Institute did it for your protection.

The facts are: 1 HP = 9,000 B.T.U.'s — 1 ton = 12,000 B.T.U.'s. It would follow then that a 1-1/3 HP unit would operate a 1 ton air conditioner. This is not necessarily true — a 1 ton air conditioning unit must (now by law) be capable of removing 12,000 B.T.U.'s from a room. A 1-1/3 HP compressor may be incapable of doing that.

For schools, where help is limited to female operators, a machine is available which requires less strength to operate.

POPULAR SCHOOL PATTIE VARIATIONS

No. Patties per Pound	Ozs.	Thickness	Diam. of Pattie
6	2.67	5/16"	4-5/16"
7	2.29	5/16"	4"
8	2.00	5/16"	3-3/4"
9	1.78	5/16"	3-9/16"
10	1.60	5/16"	3-11/32"

(Other variations with ¼" thicknesses also available.)

The average production of hand operated pattie machines is from 20 to 40 patties per minute.

To preserve the natural juices and attain smooth operation the meat should be 40⁰ F. or above.

Other styles and sizes of machines available.

BURGER OR MEATBALL MACHINES
(Electric)

Designed to produce patties or meatballs, by using plates with various diameter holes and adjusting thickness setting patties of 2"-2½" or 3" diameter, numbering from 2 to 12 per pound may be produced at rates of from 1200 to 1500 per hour. An optional automatic patty remover can increase production up to approximately 3000 patties per hour.

By using plates with hole diameters of 1" - 1¼" - 1½" or 1¾", meatballs may be produced in the same manner as patties in quantities from 3000 up to approximately 9000 per hour using the automatic remover.

The machine described has a 20 lb. capacity hopper — ⅓ HP, 115/230 volt, single phase motor and is 17" wide x 22" long x 26" high.

It is also available with a revolving hopper and stationary propeller where minimum product agitation is desirable.

Other electric machines are available, some up to 1½ HP where very high production is required. Ask your equipment salesman or write F.E.F.

BREADING MACHINES
(3 Popular sizes listed below — others available)

1. Hand operated, drum type approximately 15" x 18" can bread up to 20 lb. of chicken in 1 minute.

2. Using same drum with motorized base (115 V plug-in) approximately 15" x 24½" can bread up to 480 lbs. of chicken per hour.

3. Semi-automatic machine, 14" x 20¼" x 20½" high — operator feeds breading and product into chute at one end. Auger pushes and turns food through breading discharging it into pan at other end. (115 V. plug-in) Capacity approximately 280 lbs. of chicken per hour.

Although the above machines are rated by pounds of chicken per hour, they are equally suited for onion rings, fish, etc.

CREPE MACHINE

Size: 14" long, 8" wide, 9" high
Capacity: 4 crepes per minute
115 volt — uses heated roller controlled by thermostat.
Automatic crepe stacker available.

BREADER/SIFTER

A new manual breading/sifting work station is available. Sifting is accomplished by shaking the stainless steel screen which is removable for discarding dough balls.

Size 58" wide x 28½" deep x 52" high w/back shelf. Available without side shelves where space is limited.

Capacity 25 lbs. flour mix and 10 lbs. raw product.

DOUGHNUT SUGARING MACHINE

One model approximately 60" long, 24" wide and 36" high thoroughly coats approximately 350 dozen doughnuts per hour with any type sugar. Equipped with infeed hopper, bin to catch excess sugar at discharge end, one catch basket and knocker. Machine equipped with one drum. Extra drum is optional and may be stored under machine on brackets bolted to base. Legs are adjustable. Powered by single phase, 115V 1/3 H.P. gear head motor. Optional 220 volt, 3 phase motor available. Drums are fabricated from stainless steel and aluminum.

Optional Infeed Conveyor: Three foot long, bolts to feed end of sugar machine. Doughnuts are fed into machine on wire conveyor belt, powered by a separate gear head motor, 115 volt only.

A smaller doughnut sugaring machine, measuring only 40" in length, is available. Infeed conveyor will not operate with the smaller unit.

MANUAL DOUGHNUT GLAZER

This unit available as counter model or with mobile stand. Dip tank holds about 5 gallons of sugar glaze. Tank drain is in center front of unit. In operaton: 6 stainless steel rods are inserted into vertically spaced sockets in the back of the unit (3 each side). Doughnuts are strung on twelve rods, supplied with the unit, after dipping these rods, with doughnuts, are hung bridged across the rods extending out from the back for draining. The unit is fabricated from 16 ga. S/S, enclosed three sides and has a convenient work shelf on top.

AUTOMATIC MOBILE COOKIE DROPPER

Capable of producing a wide variety of cookies at the rate of up to 1200 dozen per hour. The machine measures 66" x 32" x 56" high. Has built-in shelf for die storage.

Features are:
- All parts in contact with dough and under the product zone are rustless:
     Stainless steel hopper
     Stainless steel table top - 22" x 65"
     Stainless steel pan guide and feed roll shafts
     Aluminum alloy feed rolls, feed chute, die holder, and dies
     Aluminum alloy cutter fingers
- Above parts easily removable without the use of tools for washing after use
- 30 quart capacity is standard - larger sizes available
- Compact fully enclosed geared in head motor unit with reduction gears running in oil bath and with direct linkage drive
- Drive gears operate feed rolls and pan belts through silent automatic clutches.
- Pans ride on two adjustable V belts
- Feed rolls are striated for positive dough feed
- Variable speed - 35-70 strokes per minute
- Adjustment knob for cookie thickness
- Adjustment knob for cookie spacing
- ½ HP, 1 phase, 115 volt, or 3 phase, 220 volt, complete with three wire 8 ft. cord with molded three prong grounding plug and adapter
- Mounted on 5" diameter ball bearing rubber tired (or plastic) casters - two swivel and two fixed
- Stainless steel - adjustable for 17" to 19" pans
- Dozens of rustless aluminum dies available. See separate die sheet

CUTTER MIXERS (VERTICAL)

Table top model 20" wide x 14" deep x 24" high. Standard accessories: shaft with narrow knives for all cutting operations, i.e. hamburg, hot dogs, bologna, vegetables, salads, cole slaw, cake batters, cheese and some salad dressings. Also yeast dough where fine textures are required. A knead/mix shaft is provided for mixing yeast dough where higher volume is desired.
Standard motor: 1 HP - 220 V. - Single phase, 10 amp.
Available: 2 HP - 220 V. - Three phase, 7 amp motor.

TYPICAL APPLICATIONS

PRODUCT	Lbs. Per Load	Time
Cookie Dough	8 lbs.	2-3 Min.
Fruit Filling	15 lbs.	1 Min.
Icing/Frosting	15 lbs.	1 Min.
Bread Crumbs	3 lbs.	1 Min.
Cole Slaw	9 lbs.	½ Min.
Mashed Potatoes (instant)	8 lbs.	½ Min.

CUTTER/MIXERS (VERTICAL)

Tilt forward type floor models — both 30 qt. and 45 qt. machines have same 23-3/8" wide x 22¼" deep base. Overall space required approximately 40" in width x 51" front to back in tilt position with cover open and 63" clear height. Both the 30 and the 45 qt. machines have 5 HP motors. Motors have dual voltage configuration - 200/60/3 or 230/460/60/3. Note 3 phase only available. Be sure to check your voltage and phase when ordering. The 200 or 230 V motor requires 30 amp service. The 460 V a 20 amp service.
Typical capacities for these are shown below.

Fig. 4-1

SOME TYPICAL PRODUCTION CAPACITIES			
Item	30 Qt. Unit	45 Qt. Unit	Time
Pizza Dough	12 to 24 lbs.	18 to 36 lbs.	2 to 3 Min.
Meat Loaf	12 to 25 lbs.	20 to 40 lbs.	1 to 2 Min.
Cole Slaw	10 to 20 lbs.	20 to 35 lbs.	30 to 45 Seconds
Mayonnaise	10 to 20 qts.	16 to 32 qts.	2 to 3 Min.
Tossed Salad	4 to 8 heads	6 to 10 heads	5 Seconds

NOTE: These machines are extremely versatile. The items listed in Fig. 4-1 represent only a few that may be processed.

Other vertical cutter/mixers are available with bowl sizes up to 120 qt. Motor speeds vary by manufacturer and some machines have two speed motors rated at 1500 and 3000 R.P.M.

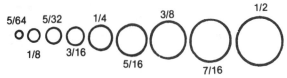

HELPFUL HINTS

A floor sink or floor drain at the point of discharge when the bowl is tilted to empty it and a wash-down hose are very handy and time saving for clean ups.

MEAT CHOPPERS OR GRINDERS

Many sizes and styles are available. Listed below is the typical production capability of various HP choppers to aid you in selecting the proper machine for your requirements.

The machines are table top models and require a space approximately 18" deep by 36" wide.

Machine Horsepower	Pounds of Meat Per Minute
1/4	5
1/2	8
1	16
2	35-40
3	35-40

NOTE: These figures are based on using plates with 1/8" dia. holes. Capacities increase substantially when using plates with larger holes.

Illustrated below are hole sizes of plates available, shown full size for handy reference.

5/64 5/32 1/4 3/8 1/2
1/8 3/16 5/16 7/16

AUTOMATIC MEAT MARINATOR

A mobile, electric plug-in unit occupying approximately 24" x 36" of floor space with a revolving, liquid-tight drum has the capacity of marinating up to 24 head of chicken or 20 lbs. of meat in one 15 minute cycle. The undershelf holds a large capacity drain tray.

BUFFALO CUTTER/CHOPPER (Spinning Bowl Type)

The spinning bowl type food cutter has been a favorite for years. Usually considered a table-top machine, some are available with a pedestal base. Models are available with 1/3 HP motors and also with or without power drive hubs for other attachments. The machines require a space approximately 33" wide x 24" deep.

Fig. 4-2

SOME APPROXIMATE PRODUCTION FIGURES FOR SPINNING BOWL FOOD CUTTERS

Item	Volume	Time
Bread Crumbs	5 lbs.	2 Min.
Cabbage	6 heads	1 Min.
Potatoes for Hash Browns	8 lbs.	1 Min.
Parsley	4 lbs.	1 Min.
Celery	6 lbs.	1 Min.
Onions	5 lbs.	1 Min.

FOOD CUTTERS (Continuous Feed)

NOTE: In general terms, Food Cutters differ from food processors in that they have a continuous feed only and the cut, grated or chopped food empties into any container of your choice. Food processors have bowls in which the food may be processed with various blades and attachments. Some processors have continuous feed attachments.

One might think of the smaller food processors as "souped-up" blendors having the advantage of larger cutting blades and the versatility of various attachments. The mid-size processors might be called little vertical cutter mixers, while the larger ones, up to 9 HP, actually are vertical cutter mixers equalling and even surpassing them in production capabilities.

HAND POWERED FOOD CUTTERS

These units clamp to table edge and allow food preparation at fairs and other locations without power requirements.

SOME TYPICAL FOOD CUTTER PRODUCTION GUIDES (Continuous Feed)

Since cheese is considered to be the most difficult product to process some machines are rated as follows:

1/3 HP Motor — 200 lbs. cheese/hr.
1/2 HP Motor — 400 lbs. cheese/hr.
3/4 HP Motor — 600 lbs. cheese/hr.
1 HP Motor — 800 lbs. cheese/hr.

jog control, for ease of unloading, a large stainless steel see thru wire forms the bowl guard; A hinged spiral arm, swings up to allow removal of bowl trolley facilitating clean up. Dimensions vary. The large model holds 350 pounds dough capacity, is 32″ wide, 54¾″ deep and 55″ high. Check voltages, weights and dimensions carefully. You may need special wiring for these high producers.

MIXER CAPACITY CHART FOR PIZZA DOUGHS

Product	20 Qt. (lbs.)	30 Qt. (lbs.)	60 Qt. (lbs.)	1½ HP 80 Qt. (lbs.)	2 HP 80 Qt. (lbs.)	140 Qt. (lbs.)
Dough, Thin Pizza (40% AR)	9*	14*	40*	55*	85*	135*
Dough, Medium Pizza (50% AR)	10*	20*	70*	90*	155*	190*
Dough, Thick Pizza	20*	40*	70#	90#	155#	190#

The %AR (% Absorption Ratio) = Water weight divided by flour weight.
*1st Speed   #2nd Speed

Fig. 4-6

APPROXIMATE MIXER DIMENSIONS

Bowl Capacity	Width	Depth	Height	Style
5 Qt.	10½″	15″	17″	Counter Model
10 qt.	14″	16″	26″	Counter Model
12 qt.	15½″	19″	27″	Counter Model
20 Qt.	15½″	21″	30″	Counter Model
20 Qt.	21″	21½″	41″	Floor Model
30 Qt.	21″	24″	45″	Floor Model
60 Qt.	27½″	39″	56″	Floor Model
80 Qt.	27½″	41½″	56″	Floor Model
140 Qt.	29½″	45½″	71½″	Floor Model

MIXER HORSEPOWER AND HUB ATTACHMENT SIZES

Fig. 4-7

Quarts	HP	Hub Size
5	1/6	#10
10	1/4	#10
12	1/4	#12
20	1/3	#12
30	1/2	#12
60	1	#22
80	1½ or 2	#22
140	5	#22

COMMON ADAPT DOWN BOWL ATTACHMENTS
(In Quart Sizes)

FROM	TO
10	3
20	12
30	20
60	30-40
80	30-40-60
140	30-40-60-80-100

COMMON ATTACHMENTS FOR MIXERS
SLICER SHREDDER AND GRATER W/PLATES
SPEED DRIVE - Increases hub speed approximately 3 times.

Dicer	Bowl Splash Cover
Meat Chopper	Bowl Extension Ring
Tray Holder	Bowl Truck and Adapters
Oil Dropper	Soup Strainers and Jackets

All mixers of course have available a wide selection of dough hooks, dough knives and whips.

For small mixers up to 20 qt., stands are available with shelves under for attachments and a tool pole at the rear corner. Locking casters optional.

For establishments requiring only the vegetable slicer or the dicer or for those who wish a separate station where slicing, grating, dicing, cutting or shredding may be done without tying up the power source of other machines, two power drive units are available.

One operates at 700 R.P.M. AND IS SUITED TO THE VEGETABLE SLICER ATTACHMENT ONLY.

The other runs at 350 R.P.M. and accommodates either the slicer or dicer attachments.

Each has 115 V - ½ HP motor and is approximately 10" wide x 20" deep x 17" high.

HAND MIXER - COMMERCIAL

This hand held mixer features a 110 volt variable speed drive assembly. The attachments are 16" in length and available as beaters, cutter, blenders and non cutting - blending for mixing only. The unit comes with a wall bracket for storage. The unit may be used for mashing potatoes, whipping cream, batters or dressings and for stirring of stews and soups.

PASTA MACHINES

A small pasta machine capable of producing 27 to 35 lbs. per hour is approximately 15" wide x 30" deep x 47" high. By changing dies it will produce typical "Bologna" pasta, sfoglia, noodles and spaghetti of different diameters. A ravioli machine is available as an attachment. The motor is 120 Volt 1½ HP.

LARGER PASTA MACHINES AVAILABLE

Fig. 4-8

| No. | OVERALL SIZE | | | Production | Voltage | Motor | Mixer |
	Width	Depth	Height	Lbs. Per Hour		HP	HP
1	25"	42"	55"	55 to 65	120/60/1	1.5	1
2	79'	39½"	79"	130 to 155	240/60/1	3	1
3	63"	54"	83'	220 to 265	240/60/1	5.5	1.5
4	98½"	54"	79"	220 to 305	240/60/1	(two) 3	1.5
5	122"	54"	83"	440 to 485	240/60/1	(two) 5.5	1.5

NOTE: Number 3 and 5 are custom.

Number 4 and 5 have two extrusion assemblies, can produce two different types of pasta at the same time.

PEELERS

Available vegetable peelers are listed below. The 1/3 HP model may be ordered as a counter model for use on a sink drainboard or with optional mobile or enclosed base with peel trap. All require electric, water and drain.

Fig. 4-9

| Item | PEELER HORSEPOWER | | |
	1/3 HP	3/4 HP	1 HP
Potatoes Peel Time	15-20 lbs. 1-3 Min.	30-33 lbs. 1-3 Min.	50-60 lbs. 1-3 Min.
Carrots Peel Time	6-12 lbs. 1-3 Min.	15-25 lbs. 1-3 Min.	Not Recommended
Beets Peel Time	10-15 lbs. 1 Min. Maximum	15-25 lbs. 1 Min. Maximum	Not Recommended

The 3/4 HP model is available with an optional base for use with a disposer unit.

PIE FORMING MACHINE

A typical 115 V - 1/4 HP counter unit - 24" wide x 19" deep x 28" high forms up to 700 (1" to 12") plain, crimped or spyder pie crust shells per hour. Other style machines will produce up to 350 top and 350 bottom shells per hour. Specialty styles available for making tarts, shells, and other snack food specialties.

PIE DOUGH ROLLERS

A typical 115 V - 1/4 HP counter pie dough roller 26" wide x 30" deep x 14" high having a 7" upper roller and 14" finishing roller with thickness adjustments is available as a counter top unit or with mobile base.
Many other styles and sizes are available

- combination pie dough roller and pastry sheeters for pie crusts, coffee cakes, buns, sweet rolls, danish, etc.
- triple-duty units for pie crusts, pastry sheeting and bread molding
- all available with various conveyor lengths and motor sizes.

PIZZA CRUST ROLLERS

The three machines listed below are available with right or left hand feed and thickness adjustment. Floor stand optional.

PIZZA ROLLER (MANUAL)

Manual pizza crust rollers:
Two manually operated pizza rollers are available featuring upper rollers ad-

Fig. 4-10

HP	Pizza Dia.	Machine Size	Top Roller	Finish Roller
1/3	9"-11" or 13"	29" x 33" x 14" high	7"	14"
1/3	10"-12" or 14"	32" x 33" x 14" high	7"	17"
1/2	12"-14" or 16"	36" x 33" x 14" high	7"	21"

Fig. 4-11

MEAT SAWS
TYPICAL SPECIFICATIONS

HP	Blade	Cutting Clearance	Movable Table	Travel	Approx. Floor Space Req'd.
1	5/8" x 98"	13-5/16" x 10-7/8" wide	15" x 20"	18"	32" x 45" deep
2 or 3	5/8" x 112"	15-1/4" x 13-1/4" wide	15" x 19"	22"	35" x 45" deep
2 or 3	5/8" x 128"	18-1/8" x 15-11/16" wide	17½" x 24"	24"	40" x 52" deep

NOTE: 1 or 2 HP motors available 115 V to 460 V - 1 or 3 phase.
3 HP high speed motor 3 phase only.

justable from 0 to ¼" for the first pass and the lower roller 0 to ⅛" for the second pass. Hand rollers produce six or more yields per minute and will form ten to sixteen inch pizza shells. The larger unit is 22" long, 10" wide and 10½" high. Add 6" to length for handle. Also available as a turnover roller for folded dough products and excellent for calzones, pierogies, baked turnovers, fried pies and more.

SLICERS

Slicers range in sizes as shown in Fig. 4-12 and specifications vary by manufacturer. One important factor to consider when purchasing is whether the slicer is gear or belt driven.

Fig. 4-12

Feed Style	Knife Diameter	Cut Thickness
Flat - Hand	9" to 10"	0" to ¾'
Angle - Hand	8" to 12"	0" to 1¾"
Angle - Automatic	10" to 12"	0" to 1¾"

STANDARD SLICER KNIVES

Slicer knives are available in diameters of 8"-9"-10"-11"-11½"-11¾" or 12".

Available optional slicer attachments:

Multiple carriage fences to hold tomatoes, etc.
Tubular chutes for celery, etc.
Stackers
Spiked holders
Heat lamps for hot roast beef, etc.

ELECTRONIC, DIGITAL AUTOMATIC PORTION CONTROL FOR SLICERS

Ideal for sandwich and deli shops, units adapt to most automatic and manual slicers and offer a remote portion control and digital read-out to 1/10th of an ounce.

Weighing unit rests on slicer receiving bed. Remote read-out and control unit automatically shuts off slicer when preselected portion weight is reached.

Available as single push button unit that can be simply re-set to any desired weight or as a unit having 4 push-button settings to meet varied portion control requirements.

OPTIONAL FEATURES: Resettable digital portion counter or non-resettable portion counter which provides a locked-in running count of total portions.

The following chart shows what small overweight errors can cost in lost profits.

Fig. 4-14

Amount Over	Period of Time	WEIGHINGS PER DAY					
		at $2.39 per lb.		at $2.99 per lb.		at $3.69 per lb.	
		100	300	100	300	100	300
1/4 oz.	Week	26.11	78.33	32.60	98.07	40.35	121.04
Over-	Month	109.66	328.98	137.30	411.90	169.47	508.41
Weight	Year	1315.92	3947.75	1647.60	4942.80	2033.64	6100.92

AUTOMATIC SLICER, CONVEYOR, STACKER

Fully automated table top slicing machine. (Stationary or mobile base available.)

Size 23" wide, 20" deep, 20" high — extended carriage and conveyor increase width to approximately 90".

Ideal for Deli or Supermarket installations. Unit is capable of producing a continuous supply of freshly cut food, either shingled (fanned out) or stacked from single pieces up to 5½" x 8-7/8" or from any combination of various items which will fit in the feed tray at one time.

Slice thickness adjustable from approx. 1/64" to 5/16". Unit has a 'last slice' attachment. Standard carriage allows slicing approximately 7¼" without reclamping — long carriage allows for slicing up to 12" without reclamping.

When the desired and preselected number of slices (up to 12 at a time) or a stack up to approx. 3¼" high has been reached the machine switches itself off automatically.

Use of the automatic conveyor belt and receiving tray in conjunction with the control panel provides many options ideally suited to large volume operations, particularly when associated with vacuum packaging.

Use F.E.F. Personal Assistance Service for further information.

HELPFUL HINTS

It is often desirable to have your slicer mobile. Stands with drop-down side shelves and angle ledge pan slides underneath are available.

TENDERIZERS

Typical size: 12" x 20" x 20" high - motor ½HP - 115V plug-in.
Knife styles: Cutting - tenderizing or cubing only
              Cutter-knitter - frozen foods
Variable feed openings. Star knives for scoring meat available.

pot and vegetable sink we suggest referring to Chapter 9 (Warewashing) where the many variables in sink construction are illustrated and described in detail. Garbage disposers can be very useful in vegetable sinks. These also are detailed in Chapter 9.

The most popular size for commercial sink compartments is 24" x 24" x 14" deep. The backsplash is usually 2" thick and the rolled edge on the ends and front usually measure 1½". Using these standards a single compartment would measure 27" side to side x 27½" front to back.

Let's stop right here and clear up a lot of confusion about standard dimensioning practices. Normally as you face a piece of equipment the width or length (depending on the proportions) is the distance from side to side — the depth is from front to back and the height, from top to bottom; i.e., a standard electric range is considered 36" wide, 38" deep and 36" high. A standard restaurant range would measure 5'-0" wide x 32" deep x 36" high.

Sinks, especially die stamped drop-ins, are the confusing exceptions since the depth of a sink is quite naturally considered the vertical dimension of the part that holds the water. The distance from front to back becomes the width and side to side becomes the length, even though it may be shorter than the width.

Shelving is another less confusing exception.

Now back to sinks — the less expensive method of constructing 2 or 3 compartment sinks is with a single thickness of metal dividing the compartments (these may be N.S.F. approved). To figure the overall length of one of this construction add 3" to the sum of the length of the number of compartments; i.e., the overall length of a 24" x 24" three compartment sink would be 3 times 24" (72") plus 3" for the rolled edges (75").

The preferred method of construction is to have each compartment with fully coved inside corners. These are usually constructed with a 1" space between each compartment. Don't forget that 1" when figuring overall lengths. See Page 300-301 for illustration.

SOME POPULAR SINK COMPARTMENTS

Length (Side to Side)		Width (Front to Back)
18"	x	18"
18"	x	21"
18"	x	24"
24"	x	21"
24"	x	24"
30"	x	21"
30"	x	24"
30"	x	30"
36"	x	24"
36"	x	30"

Standard depths — 14" & 16". Others are available.

As mentioned, dimensions and details vary with each manufacturer. Use our charts to guide you but check your suppliers' dimensions if you have a tight fit.

DRAINBOARDS

Once again refer to Chapter 9 for details of construction. Here it will suffice to say that drainboards to fit any width sink are made in standard lengths of 18", 24", 30" and 36". They may be in integral part of the sink or removable. Any drainboard exceeding 36" should have its own support legs at the end.

HELPFUL HINTS

There are many options for standard sinks and those for custom sinks are almost limitless. As with any equipment, when you are shopping for prices be certain of the options and quality you want and that all bids incorporate these items.

Some options to standard sinks are:

14 or 16 gauge metal
430 or 302 stainless steel
Interconnected waste lines
Lever handle or basket wastes
Sink heaters for sanitizing
Stand pipes
Inter-connected overflows
Number of faucets
Soap Holders
Pylon style base

Sink covers
Strainer baskets
Type of gussets
Painted, S.S. clad or S.S.
   tubular legs
White metal, stainless or
   flanged feet
Leg crossbracing
Overshelves

With just a few words of caution we will end the chapter on vegetable sinks and hope you found it more informative than boring.

For sanitation purposes and ease of cleaning, sinks should be set 3" from or sealed to the wall. Shut-off valves are recommended for the water lines. Water and drain lines brought out from the wall make clean-up much easier. Be **sure** drain lines are low enough, especially if you are installing a disposer. Where possible be sure a switch mounting bracket be provided for disposers. Be sure you have enough faucets and consider fast flow faucets for large sinks. Much time can be wasted waiting for sinks to fill. Lastly, consider high end splashes when sinks are in corners or next to high items like refrigerators.

STAINLESS STEEL INGREDIENT BINS

Available with all cove corner body on base with full perimeter bumper and swivel casters.

Fig. 4-16

Capacity	Size
100 lb.	12¾" x 22" x 29" high
150 lb.	17½" x 22" x 29" high
200 lb.	20" x 22" x 29" high
250 lb.	23" x 25" x 29" high

OPTIONS: Full sliding, hinged in center or half sliding covers.

STANDARD WORK TABLES

What may be considered standard work tables and optional components (variable by manufacturers) are listed below.
All are 34" high to working surface.

Standard Widths		Standard Lengths
18" - 24" or 30"	x	3'-4'-5'-6'-7' or 8'

Stainless steel tops are usually 14 gauge with roll-down edges and bullnose corners.

Maple top tables are usually 1¾" or 3" thick. Either S/S or maple tables may have back and, or end splashes in varying heights from 1½" to 12".

Tool drawers are available with either S/S, galv. or plastic bowls in 15" x 20" x 5" or 20" x 20" x 5" sizes. They may be open type construction with channel slides or be semi-enclosed or totally enclosed with roller bearing glides. Locks may also be provided.

AVAILABLE OPTIONS FOR STANDARD WORK TABLES

Sinks
Lazy Susan pot racks
Pan slide cabinets
  (for 18" x 26" pans) - may be
  mounted on table top
  or bottom shelf
Enclosed drawer tiers

Extra angle iron, channel or hot
  channel bracing under top
Painted, S/S clad or S/S Tubular
  legs
White metal or S/S feet
Locking casters
Drip troughs for coffee urns

MOBILE PREPARATION TABLE
For Hamburg, Specialty Sandwich or Pizza Assembly

Units are 31½" H x 28¼" W and either 52" or 72" long. 14 ga. stainless steel heated top has crumb chute and drawer. 52" unit holds seven 1/6 size ice chilled pans and three 5" round pans. 72" unit holds eight 1/6 size and two 5" round pans. An optional 3 tier bun rack adds 19" to length. Units are 115 V - 52" model is 135 W. 72" model is 250 W.

Companion mobile unit to hold front return conveyor broiler and toaster is available.

POT RACKS

Common pot racks, either table mounted or ceiling hung, usually have one perimeter bar with a center bar approximately 1 ft. lower. Wall mounted pot racks are available with single bars or with 2 bars, one extending out from the wall above the other. Standard lengths are 48"-60"-72"-84" and 96". Double pot hooks hang over the bars and may be spaced as required.

A single pole merry-go-round pot rack with a round utensil shelf is available for mounting on existing work tables.

The recommended height to the top bar of a pot rack is 7'-6" above the floor.

STANDARD STAINLESS STEEL OVERHEAD SHELVES

Standard widths of shelves are 10"-12"-18" or 24". Standard lengths are 48"-60"-72"-84"-96" or 108". Standard metal gauges used are 18 - 16 or 14.

Naturally the wider and longer the shelf the heavier the metal should be.

The shelving may be ordered for either single or double table mounting. Standard spacing for shelving is 18" from the table top to the first shelf with 12" between shelves.

Standard wall hung shelves are available in the same gauges and sizes as above.

HELPFUL HINTS

Always give careful consideration to the weight of items you intend to place on shelving making certain that the supports are properly spaced. Extra bracing under the shelves may be required. If you intend to have electrical equipment on or under the shelves, such as heat lamps, the wiring may often be run up inside of the support tubing.

The authors cannot over emphasize the importance of making certain that there is ample support in a wall before ordering any wall hung unit.

AVERAGE B.T.U. RATINGS FOR COOKING EQUIPMENT (Cont.)
(The low to high rating will depend on final selection.)

		B.T.U.
STEAMERS	Compartment	40,000-225,000
OVENS	Convection, Counter	35,000 Average
	Full Size	75,000-115,000
	Deck Ovens, per deck	30,000-240,000
	Pizza, per deck	50,000-140,000

NOTE: Sizes of these pieces of equipment and their capacities will be found further ahead in this chapter.

TYPICAL PREHEAT TIMES — GAS EQUIPMENT

Broilers - Radiant	15-20 min.
Infrared	1 min.
Branding Grills	20-30 min.
Char Broilers	20 min.
Grills	20-30 min.
Fryers	10-12 min.
Fry Pan Tilt	5- 7 min.
Hot Top Range	20-30 min.
Ovens - Convection 350°	10-15 min.
Ovens - Deck	30-60 min.
Ovens - Range	15-30 min.
Steamer - Compartment	5-15 min.
Steam Kettle	10-20 min.

Steamers and kettles will vary with type of heat generation.

TYPICAL KW RATINGS FOR ELECTRIC COOKING EQUIPMENT
(Sizes and production will be discussed further on in this chapter.)

ITEM		K.W.
BROILERS	Counter	12
	Upright	12 to 32
	Char Type, 2 ft.	8
	Char Type, 3 ft.	12
FRYERS	Small	4.5 to 5.5
	Medium	12
	Large	22

(Continued)

TYPICAL KW RATINGS FOR ELECTRIC COOKING EQUIPMENT (Cont.)
(Sizes and production will be discussed further on in this chapter.)

ITEM		K.W.
FRYERS, PRESSURE		
	Counter Style	6
	Floor Style	11
GRILLS		6 to 32
TILT FRY PAN		7.5 to 21
STEAM KETTLE 5 Gal. to 100 Gal.		6 to 18
COMPARTMENT STEAMER		24 to 48
PIZZA OVENS	Counter	1.8 to 3.5
	Deck - One	7.5
	Two	14
	Three	21
CONVECTION OVENS		
	Counter	5.6
	Full Size Per Section	11
DECK OVENS		7 to 11 per deck
RANGES	Top Burners	11 to 16
	Ovens Below	6

TYPICAL PREHEAT TIMES FOR ELECTRIC COOKING EQUIPMENT

BROILERS.............................. 15-20 min.

FRYERS............................ Average 6 min.

GRILLS - to 325⁰.......................... 5-8 min.

TILT FRY PAN............................ 10 min.

*STEAM KETTLE......................... 10-15 min.

*COMPARTMENT STEAMER............... 10-15 min.

*Will vary on boiler - pressure and KW load.

OVENS
      Range................................. 20 min.
      Deck.................... 40 min. average deck
      Convection.......................... 9-10 min.

RANGES
      Hot Top................................ 50 min.
      French Top............................ 30 min.
      Open Burners .... 5 min.

TYPICAL SIZES ELECTRIC BROILERS

DESCRIPTION	W"	D"	H"	KW
1 Section Counter	36	34-3/8	34	12
1 Section on 1-pan oven	36	38-1/4	64	18
1 Section on convection oven	36	38-1/4	64	18.8
1 Section on cabinet base	36	38	64	12
2 Sections on 1-pan oven	36	38-1/4	78	30
2 Sections on convection oven	36	38-1/4	78	30.8
2 Sections on cabinet base	36	38	78	24

UPRIGHT ELECTRIC BROILERS
(Typical Size and Load - 1 Section Production)

OVERALL SIZE: 36" x 36" x 67" high
GRID SIZE: 25" wide x 22½" deep

Item	Product Weight	Production Per Hour
Strip Steak	¾ lb.	124 hr.
Chicken Halves	1 lb.	36 hr.
Lobster Tails	¾ lb.	236 hr.

NOTE: Using square inch of grid and square inch of product divide for actual load.

$$
\begin{array}{r}
\text{Above grid} \quad 25 \\
\underline{22} \\
50 \\
\underline{50} \\
550 \text{ Sq. Inches}
\end{array}
$$

Strip Steak 3" x 8" = 24 sq. inches

$$
\begin{array}{r}
22 \\
24 \overline{)550} = \text{Approx. 22 per load} \\
\underline{48} \\
70
\end{array}
$$

BROILED FOODS DONENESS GUIDE

Description	Product Is
Rare	Wide, deep red center
Medium Rare	Deep red center
Medium	Deep pink center
Medium Well	Light pink center
Well Done	Brown center

COMPARATIVE TIME CHART FOR GAS BROILERS

Food Item	Char Broil	Radiant Broil	Infra Red
1'' Thick Steak	8-9 min.	8-9 min.	4 min.
1½'' Thick Steak	12-14 min.	13-15 min.	6½ min.
2'' Thick Steak (med. rare)	16-20 min.	18-20 min.	8-9 min.
¼ lb. Burger	4 min.	4 min.	2 min.
½'' Thick Burger	5 min.	5 min.	3 min.
¾'' Thick Burger (med. rare)	7 min.	8 min.	4 min.
¾'' Chop (well)	7-8 min.	6-7 min.	3-4 min.

ELECTRIC BROILING GUIDE

MEAT	THICKNESS (Inches)	Total Time, Minutes (One-half time on each side)		
		RARE	MEDIUM	WELL DONE
BEEF				
Rib Steak	1	6-8	8-10	10-12
Club Steak	1	6-8	8-10	10-12
Porterhouse......................	1	6-8	8-10	10-12
Porterhouse......................	1½	8-10	11-13	14-16
Porterhouse......................	2	10-12	13-15	16-18
Sirloin	1	6-8	8-10	10-12
Sirloin	1½	8-10	11-13	14-16
Sirloin	2	10-12	13-15	16-18
Ground Beef Patties...............	¾	3-4	4-6	6-8
Tenderloin	1	6-8	8-10	10-12
LAMB				
Rib or Loin Chops (1 rib)	¾	—	8-10	10-12
Double Rib.......................	1½	—	11-13	14-16
Lamb Shoulder Chops	¾	—	8-10	10-12
Lamb Shoulder Chops	1½	—	11-13	14-16
Lamb Patties.....................	¾	—	4-6	6-8
HAM AND SAUSAGE				
Ham Slices	½	—	—	6-8
Ham Slices	'¼	—	—	8-10
Ham Slices	1	—	—	10-12
Sausage Links (12/lb.)	—	—	—	4-5
BROILING CHICKENS				
Halves (1½ lb.)	—	—	—	18-22

CHAR STYLE BROILING CHART AND TIMING GUIDE

		Minutes Each Side		
Item	**Thick**	**Rare**	**Med.**	**Well**
Porterhouse	1"	6	8	10
T-Bone - Club	1½"	9	10	13
Sirloin	2"	12	16	—
Hamburg	½"	2	4	6
CHICKEN			**Done**	
Broiling Chicken	¾ lb.		9 min.	
Ready ½ chickens	1 lb.		11 min.	
	1½ lb.		14 min.	
PORK				
Chops	1"		15-20 min.	
Spare Ribs			20-30 min.	

ELECTRIC CHAR BROIL LOAD & PRODUCTION GUIDE

Grid Size	Product	Per Load	Per Hr.
15 x 22	Hamburg	24	340
	Strip Steak	9	80
16 x 20	Hamburg	24	380
	Strip Steak	12	90
20 x 32	Hamburg	48	760
	Strip Steak	24	180

(Medium doneness)
Hamburg 2½ oz.
N.Y. Strip 8 x 3 x ½"

MESQUITE CHARCOAL BROILERS

A popular wood burning broiler, normally built with a well insulated hearth brick fire box and ceramic walls, is available for Mesquite wood broiling. A typical floor style dimension sheet follows. Counter and built-in styles are also available.

DIMENSIONAL SPECIFICATIONS

Width	30¼"	36¼"	48¼"
Depth	27"	27"	27"
Height at back & sides (with legs)	40"	40"	40"
Working height of grid—2 positions (with legs)	35" & 39"	35" & 39"	35" & 39"
Cooking area top grid	575 Sq. In.	713 Sq. In.	989 Sq. In.
Top grid size(s)	24¾ × 26¾	PR. 24¾ × 16³⁄₁₆ ea.	PR. 24¾ × 22⅜ ea.
Firebox (inside dimensions)	20 × 21½ × 9	20 × 27½ × 9	20 × 39½ × 9
Utility drawers (1 ash drawer, 1 storage)	2 drawers each 13 × 9½ × 25	2 drawers each 16 × 9½ × 25	2 drawers each 16 × 9½ × 25
Shipping Weight	470 lbs.	570 lbs.	710 lbs.

ROTISSERIE STYLE ELECTRIC BROILER

SIZE: 24" wide, 21" deep, 21" high. Rated at 3.2 KW, 208/220 — 250 hamburgs per hour.

NOTE: Check local codes. This rotisserie style cooker may not need venting.

BROILER, ELECTRIC
CONVEYOR - TWO TRACKS

208 or 230V, 1 or 3 phase, 9.9 KW

COUNTER TOP STYLE

SIZE: 42" to 60" x 20" x 22" high

TUNNEL STYLE: Dual controls allow the operator to choose speed for each track.

PRODUCTS: Hamburgs, buns, hot dogs, sausage patties and sandwich steaks.

Approximate Hamburger Production

Patty Size	Food Temp.	Thickness	Per Hr. Production
10 to lb.	40°F	3/16	675
4 to lb.	40°F	5/16	240
10 to lb.	0°F	3/16	300
4 to lb.	0°F	5/16	125

Food temperature end of cook cycle 150°.

MOBILE BROILERS FOR OUTSIDE USE
(on Trailer Style Wheels)

Styles available include L.P. gas, charcoal or wood fired.

FACTS:

102" long x 48" wide x 33" high

Broiler Grates: 2 - 32½ x 26¼ S/S

Griddles: 2 - 32½ x 26¼ cast

LP Gas Tanks: 2 - 20 lb. capacity each

BTU's: 74,000

Automatic pilot light, thermostat and shut off valve.

Trailer has standard 1-7/8" hitch, lights and plate brackets

A 6'-6" serving table slides out to form work/serve area. Covers cook area when not in use.

er cavity. Single drawer units 110/220 Volt — 2 drawer units 208 - 220/240 Volt. Both units 18½" deep x 16½" high. Single 21" wide - double unit 33½" wide, thermostat control, cord and plug supplied.

Check local codes — may not require venting. Able to produce six one quarter pound hamburgers per drawer, 3½ to 4 minutes from a refrigerated state.

FRYER FACTS - ELECTRIC AND GAS

STYLES AVAILABLE:
1) Conventional gas and electric counter and floor models
2) Computerized Fryers
3) Pressure Fryers
4) Conveyor high production types
5) Specialty Fryers - donut, high BTU chicken and fish models
6) Fryers are now available with built in automatic filter systems. Also available are fryers with automatic temperature controls, (no thermostats)
7) Air Pressure - new style fryer uses no oil. Further information not available at this time.

FRYER FACTS - BRAINSTORMING

1) Mobile
2) Automatic lifts
3) Computer timers
4) Computer controls
5) Fat melt cycle
6) Test alert system
7) Quick disconnects
8) Drop in
9) Counter
10) Free standing
11) Full or half baskets
12) Ease of cleaning
13) Ease of draining
14) Ease of filtering
15) Dual pots in same housing
16) Simmer cover - gives O pressure frying
17) Apron drain, attaches to side of fryer
18) Spreader - separates 2 fryers or fryer from other equipment
19) Crumb tray
20) Element style if electric

FAT FILTERS

Some french fry units are available with built-in filtering systems. The filtering system may be contained within the fryer or added to the side. The filtering may be continual or in cycles.

Separate, mobile fat filters are available in sizes from approximately 50 lb. to 250 lb. capacities. Each manufacturer offers certain desirable features such as, filter papers or powders, purification cartridges, fat melting capacities, reversible pumps, etc.

Typical Fat Filtering Units

Drum Dia.	Fat Capacity	
	Pounds	Gallons
17"	60	8
17"	120	16½
20"	150	20
20"	250	33-1/3

Above models rated as 5.5 Amp., 110 V., 1/4 H.P.

Manual filters using cotton fiber or reusable, washable filters are normally sufficient for small counter fryers.

Potential savings from proper handling and filtering can be significant. Take a few minutes to read the following "FAT FACTS"

FRYER FAT DECOMPOSITION
(Approximate Temperature Breakdown)

Product	Breakdown Temp.
Corn & Cottonseed Oil	430° - 475°
Hydrogenated Oils	430° - 475°
Lard	385° - 430°
Butter	405°
Olive Oil	333° - 347°

SMOKING TEMPERATURES OF VARIOUS FATS

Hydrogenated	440° - 460°	Lard	340° - 350°
Standard Vegetable	420° - 440°	Olive Oil	300° - 315°
Cottonseed Oil	410° - 430°	Bacon Fat	290° - 300°
Corn Oil	400° - 430°	Beef Suet	235° - 245°
Chicken Fat	400° - 430°		

FAT FACTS

Fresh frying fat requires a certain amount of breaking-in or degredation to make it a suitable cooking medium. This process commences when it is first brought up to frying temperature but unfortunately cannot be stopped when the fat reaches the point where it yields fine foods lightly colored and flavored and have a crisp exterior but still remain moist inside. Fat breakdown is caused by heat, air and chemicals from the foods cooked in it.

Fat will change its chemical properties even without the introduction of food due to being heated in the atmosphere. The physical properties of the fat change which lowers its surface tension and increases its viscosity. This changes the heat transfer and soaking properties of the fat.

Antioxidants and antifoamers cannot stop the gradual degradation process, but the useful life of the fat can be maximally extended when —

1. Frequent and effective filtering is employed for partical removal.
2. "Oil cleaning" or treatment is carried out for soluble contaminants.
3. When high volumes of foods are produced in relatively low volumes of fat. This carries away much of the "old fat". When replacement fat is one third of the total fat in the fryer, the quality life cycle can be materially extended.

Soap is an enemy of frying fat. Pioneers produced their own soap by cooking an alkaline product with fat. Soap is produced in the frying fat when the alkaline food juices combine with the free fatty acids in the frying fat. Test chemicals, to show soap content and oil cleaning chemicals and effective filtration systems are available

The fast recovery of high B.T.U. input fryers allows lower frying temperatures. The burner running time is less and preheating is faster. Gas fryers are available with standing pilots or spark ignition. Several states have legislation to outlaw standing pilots. Check your state requirements.

TYPICAL ELECTRIC FRYERS
(Sizes and Production)

OIL CAPACITY (LBS.)	FRENCH FRIES/HR.		KW	PREHEAT TO 350F (MINUTES)	WATTS TO HOLD 350F	OVERALL BODY DIMENSIONS		
						W	D	H (LESS LEGS)
15	27 lbs. raw-to-done		5.5	6	485	17-31/32	20	12-5/16
15	27 lbs. raw-to-done		5.5	6	485	17-31/32	22-1/2	12-5/16
28	2-oz. blanched servings	600	12	6	770	21-1/2	25-5/32	13-3/8
28		600	12	6	770	25-1/2	25-5/32	13-3/8
28		600	12	6	770	20	38	35
28		600	12	6	770	20	38	35
28		600	12	6	770	20	38	22-1/2
28		600	12	6	770	20	38	22-1/2
28		600	12	6	770	20	38	35
30	56 lbs. raw-to-done		11.4	9.5	770	24-4/5	23-1/2	14-5/16
50	50 lbs. frozen fish filets		11	7*	836	15-5/8	28	34-1/2
50	100 lbs. blanched-to-done		16.5	5*	836	15-5/8	28	34-1/2
60	90 lbs. fried chicken		18	10	1300	24	38	35
60	90 lbs. fried chicken		18	10	1300	24	38	22-1/2

SUPER HEATED HOT AIR COOKER (ELECTRIC)

A unique device that cooks and reconstitutes foods by using constantly circulating super heated air around the food. The air circulating blower forces air across an electric calrod heater and into the cooking cavity. A revolving perforated drum circulates the air throughout the cavity. Exhaust air is recirculated, reducing moisture loss during the cook process. Reduced ventilation costs, no fat or oils and a variety of cooking modes, makes this device a viable option to standard equipment.

Model (Specifications):

Small—14″ wide, 23″ deep, 25″ high, 2,000 Watts
Medium—25″ wide, 25″ deep, 16½″ high, 2,000 Watts
Large—26¼″ wide, 33″ deep, 40½″ high, 8,000 Watts

	Cooking Time (mins.)	Reheat Time (mins.)
French Fries	2–6	1
Onion Rings	3	1
Hamburger	4	2
Pizza 8"	3–4½	1½
Chicken, 3 piece Frozen	8–10	4
Fish, Breaded Frozen	6	1–2
Potato Skins, Frozen Processed	2–4	1
Pastry (Proofed Product)	4–7	1
Crab, Fresh	4–5	1
Scallops, Fresh	2–3½	1
Shrimp, Fresh	2–3½	1
Corn, Fresh	4½	2½
Lobster, Fresh	5	*
Steak N.Y., Broiled 1¼" thick	7½–8	3
Baked Alaska	2	*
Shish Kabob	4	1½–2
Nachos	1–1½	1
Vegetables, Battered Frozen	6	2

DONUT FRYERS · TYPICAL PRODUCTION

ELECTRIC

Size			Fat Capacity	DONUTS	
Width	Depth	KW	lbs.	Per Load	Per Hour
13"	13"	1.8	11	12	16 dz.
15"	16"	2.4	16	18	25 dz.
20"	20"	5.5	30	24	50 dz.
21"	22"	8	50	36	65 dz.
25"	26"	11	85	60	100 dz.

LARGER GAS DONUT FRYERS

Fat Capacity	BTU	Dz. Donuts Per Hr.
105/120	120,000	60
105/165	150,000	130
195	180,000	160

Also available are automated style fryers with built-in dropping and turning systems for donuts.

LOW PRESSURE FRYER

Top cover operates on 3/4 pound pressure rather than normal 13 pounds high pressure. This unit features automatic lift, front work or landing tray - capacity 1 lb. to 15 lbs. Frying time is same. Immersion basket is round. Power requirements not available at this time.

Features:
- Tone alarms
- Light signals
- Crisp controls
- Test switches for fryer and computer
- Programmable by operator changing time chips
- Holding timer
- Probe test switch
- Switch to manual timer in case of computer failure

The basic difference between solid state timer units and computer units is that timers do not have probes. Computerized control units have probes to monitor all necessary functions of the fryer.

FAT TRANSFER TRUCK

A Unique Fat Transport Truck is available to transfer fat from a fryer to grease dumpster area. A safe and unique design, allows positioning the container under fryer drain and will hold approximately 50 pounds of fat. Light weight and easy to clean makes this container very popular for volume users. (Size 35" high, 8" deep and 12" wide; weight is 16 pounds.) Also available, a unit with hand operated syphon pump.

GAS GRIDDLES

Gas industry research has introduced major breakthroughs with griddles. In recent years, it has developed the infrared griddle and the pulse griddle. Infrared griddles are 48-60 percent more efficient than gas griddles. The infrared effect is created when gas and air are mixed and forced through portholes in ceramic plates. The process yields temperatures up to 1600°F. Infrared research has also allowed manufacturers to create better zoned heating areas on the griddle surface. As a result, cooks can be more confident when simultaneously cooking two products that require different temperatures.

The new pulse griddles promise 70 percent efficiency. Gas is ignited in a combustion chamber directly beneath the griddle plate. The first pulse is ignited by a spark, subsequent gas pulses ignite automatically from heat generated from the first. The process is similar to that of a diesel car. These little explosions of gas cause a "scrubbing" effect on the griddle, greatly improving the heat transfer process. The griddle is divided into six sections with individual combustion chambers under each section. Each chamber has its own thermostatic control.

GRILLS · GRIDDLES

Defined, a grill would have top and bottom heat. This style has been used for grilled cheese sandwiches for years. Griddles were defined as bottom heat only. For this section we will consider both the same and move on to the facts.

Even though the term sandwich grill seems to stick with us, the author tends to think in terms of the cooking appliance as being the griddle and what is accomplished with it as grilling. No one ever orders a "griddled cheese sandwich".

WHEN YOUR ELECTRIC GRIDDLE IS NEW . . .

1) Use the manufacturer's operating manual that came with your griddle. Write for a new manual if yours is missing. Study the manual, then file it in a safe place for ready reference.
2) Check the nameplate on the griddle to satisfy yourself that the voltage and current characteristics match your electrical service. If in doubt, consult your local electric utility company.
3) Have your griddle installed and connected by a competent electrical contractor. Call your electric utility company if you need help.
4) Clean off the rust preventive compound applied by factory. Use a cloth dampened with a grease solvent. Wipe with a clean, damp cloth. Dry thoroughly.
5) After thorough cleaning, the grid plate must be seasoned. Preheat to 400°F. Apply a light film of unsalted cooking oil. Alow to stand for two minutes, then wipe clean. Repeat this process. Thoroughly wipe off excess oil. Your new griddle is now ready for use.

CORRECT OPERATING CARE ELECTRIC GRIDDLES

Turn dial to required temperature (reached when signal light goes out).

With machines having more than one control dial, make sure you know exactly how much of the cooking surface each control serves. Some models also feature separate perimiter control. (Consult the manufacturer's manual or your local electric utility company.)

Load and cook according to recipe. Unless the food product contains fat (e.g. bacon), the grid surface must be grease-filmed before each cooking operation.

Turn foods halfway through cooking time unless otherwise specified in recipe.

Griddle-grills, with independently controlled upper grid, cook both sides at once. (One manufacturer recommends that the upper grid should be approximately 50°F. higher than lower grid temperature to obtain desired browning and doneness.)

After each cooking load, scrape excess food and fat particles off the grid surface with a flexible spatula or wire brush.

During traffic lulls reduce temperature to "idle" (around 200°F.).

At the end of each day's operation, thoroughly clean grid, re-season and turn all temperature controls to OFF.

ELECTRIC GRIDDLE CAPACITIES
(By Griddle Size and Square Inches)

Griddle Size 15" x 18" - 266 Square Inches

Food Product	Per Load	Per Hour
Hamburger	20	300
Eggs	19	320
Pancakes	12	216

Griddle Size 15" x 30" - 445 Square Inches

Hamburger	32	480
Eggs	32	550
Pancakes	28	500

Griddle Size 18" x 24" - 429 Square Inches

Hamburger	30	'510
Eggs	28	560
Pancakes	25	375

Griddle Size 18" x 36" - 645 Square Inches

Hamburger	45	765
Eggs	42	840
Pancakes	38	570

GAS GRIDDLES - TYPICAL SIZES AND BTU'S

Usable Grill Area	B.T.U.'S
18" x 24"	45,000
18" x 36"	65,000
18" x 48"	105,000
24" x 36"	90,000
24" x 48"	138,000

HIGH HEAT TRANSFER GRIDDLES
3/4" PLATE TYPICAL B.T.U.'S OR KW

Overall Size	Griddle Size	B.T.U.'S	KW
27" x 30"	24" x 30"	80,000	7.2
30" x 30"	27" x 30"	80,000	7.2
36" x 30"	33" x 30"	80,000	10.8
42" x 30"	39" x 30"	120,000	14.4
48" x 30"	45" x 30"	160,000	14.4
60" x 30"	57" x 30"	200,000	18.0
71" x 30"	69" x 30"	240,000	21.6

Available 24" x 36" deep also.

ELECTRIC TEPPANYAKI GRIDDLES
For Oriental Steakhouse Restaurants

Complete unit is 58" x 96" x 29½" high. Seats eight comfortably. Cooking plate is 24" x 60" with two elements, thermostats, lights and switches. 208-240 Volt. Available without table.

MINI COUNTER GRIDDLE - HEAT ABOVE AND BELOW

SIZE: Varies by manufacturer. Solid plate top hinges and lays down on top of food. Also available with ribbed or groove plate.

Food Product	Per Load	Minutes to Cook 115V	220V
3/4" Steak	4	3	2
Grilled Sandwich	6	1½	1
Hot Dogs	12	3	2
Sausage Links	18	3	2
French Toast	6	1¼	1
1/2" Swordfish	4-6	6	4
3/8" Ham Steak	4-6	3	2
3 oz. Hamburg	6	1½	1

HIGH SPEED, PORTABLE GRIDDLE

Specifications: 7¼" high, 21½" wide, 14¾" deep, 115 V or 230 A.C., 1725 Watts, plug-in unit, weight 22 lbs. Cooking surface 11" x 21" heavy cast aluminum. Elements, infra-red, radiant type.

Features: Automatic thermostatic temp. control from 150° to 400°F, fast recovery, wide drain lip with grease drawer.

Application: Food demonstrations, rathskellers, terraces, luncheonettes and as stand-by units for restaurants, hotels.

VAPOR GRILL

A Char Grill style Broiler, grills meats and seafood on rapid heating stainless steel grilling elements over a humidity building water tray. This creates a seared cooked product with little moisture or weight loss. Trapping grease in the water tray eliminates flareup. Self cleaning elements clean quickly. Typical sizes:

Service	Voltage	Wattage	Width	Depth	Height	Grill Area
Single phase	115	1800	10.5"	21.5"	5.2"	5.9" × 14.3"
Single phase	208	1600	267mm	545mm	132mm	150mm × 363mm
Single phase	240	1500				
Single phase	208	3200	17"	21.5"	5.2"	12.4" × 14.3"
Single phase	240	3000	432mm	545mm	132mm	315mm × 363mm
Single phase	208	4800	23.5"	21.5"	5.2"	18.8" × 14.3"
Three phase	240	4500	597mm	545mm	132mm	477mm × 363mm

COOKING GUIDE

	Heat Setting	Cook Time— Approx. Minutes
Fish	2.75	9
Shell Fish	3	12
T-Bone (12 oz.)	2.5	9
Thick Steak	2	14
Chicken (16 oz.)	2.5	15

SOME AVAILABLE SIZES
(Standard Convection Ovens)

Power Requirements: Electric or gas range of KW from 5.5 to 37 KW. Average full size oven — 11 KW. Gas BTU's from 40,000 to 120,000. Fan motors from 1/2 to 2 HP at 1750 R.P.M.

Pan Sizings: See charts for total loads and temperatures. Full size ovens accommodate one 18" x 26" per shelf, or two 12" x 20" pans or six 9" pie pans per shelf. Please see index for product and serving ratings for these pans.

SELECTION GUIDES CONVECTION OVENS

Meals Served

50 to 100	1 - 1/2 size convection oven
100 to 400	1 - Full convection oven
400 to 750	1 - Double convection oven
750 up	1 - Double convection oven plus 1 single convection oven

From 750 meals up, consideration should be given to mobile roll in or drive in style ovens.

PAN CAPACITIES 18" x 26" PANS
(As rated for full size convection oven)

Food Item	Per Pan	Number of Shelves	Total Oven Load
Rolls	5 dz. - 1¼ oz.	4	240 rolls
Sheet Cake	70 cut	6	420 pieces
Cookies	1½ - #24 scoop	6	144
Hamburgs	24 - 3 oz.	11	264
Baked Lobster	20 lbs.	4	64¼ lbs.
Baked Potatoes	40-80	4-6	160-360

See next chart for more production figures.

OTHER CAPABILITIES

Item	No. of Pieces	Estimated Roasting Time	Oven Temp. Degrees F.
Leg of Lamb, boned and tied	85-100	4-4½ hrs.	235-250
Lamb shoulder, boned and tied	125-150	3-3½ hrs.	225-235
Canadian backs (boneless pork loin)	30-32	2½-3½ hrs.	235-250
Fresh ham, boned, rolled and tied	30-35	4-4½ hrs.	235-250
Fresh pork shoulder, boned, rolled and tied	50-65	3-3½ hrs.	235-250
*Spare ribs (brush with BBQ sauce)	200-220	2 hrs.	235-250
Chicken halves	168	2 hrs.	255-270
Chicken quarters	320-340	1½-2 hrs.	255-270
Duck halves	120-140	2-2½ hrs.	235-250
Frozen Fish Fillets	500	1-1¼ hrs.	225-250
10" x 12" Retort Pouches (at room temperature)	30	1¼ hrs.	225 - 250
Pre-cooked frozen entrees		2-3 hrs.	225-250

HALF SIZE CONVECTION OVEN
COOKING GUIDE

	Cooking Time	Number of Shelves	Number Size Portion	Portions per Hour
MEAT, FISH, POULTRY				
Baked Stuffed Lobster	10-15 min.	2	1½ #	20
Chicken Breasts	40-50 min.	3	8 oz.	30-35
Cornish Hens	45-60 min.	2	8-10 oz.	24
Meatballs	30-45 min.	3	1½ oz.	100
Roast Sirloin	1-2 hrs.*	1-3	4 oz.	60-150*
BAKED GOODS				
Danish Pastry	12-15 min.	3	1½ oz.	15 doz.
Puff Pastry	25 min.	2	4 oz.	32
Mini Loaves	12-15 min.	2	7 oz.	6 doz.
Pies - Frozen	1 hr.	3	8" pies	9 pies
Pies - Meringue	5-7 min.	2	10" pies	25 pies
MISCELLANEOUS				
Pizza	10-12 min.	3	2 oz.	175
Grilled Cheese Sandwich	8-11 min.	3	1 each	180

*60-150 portions in 1-2 hrs. depending on size of roast(s).

COUNTER ELECTRIC CONVECTION OVEN - GRID STYLE

Overall size: 24" wide, 25" deep, 29" high, using 6.5 KW. Unit will hold 6 1/2 size steam table pans, 1¼" deep or 8 - 1/3 pans 2½" deep or 4 - 2/3 size pans 2½" deep or you may roast directly on grid. For school lunch system 6½" x 5" pre pack meals the capacity per load is 24.

TYPICAL CAPACITY AND COOKING TIME
Capacity and Cooking Time — Single Oven

Dishes	Cooking time in min.	Pieces on pan	No. of pans	Charges per hour	Output per hour
Hamburgers	15	8	6	4	192 pieces
Cutlets or Chops	12	6	6	5	180 pieces
Liver	6	6	6	12	360 pieces
Sausages, large	9	6	6	6	216 pieces
Steaks	8	6	6	7	252 pieces
Fish Fillets	12	6 6	6	5	
Whole Chlicken (approx. 2½ lb.)	40	3	3	1½-2	18 pieces
Pork Roast	60	1	3	1	15 kg (33 lbs.)
Beef Roast	30	1	3	2	30 kg (66 lbs.)
Bread Rolls	17	12	3	3	108 pieces
Danish Pastries	10	10	6	6	360 pieces

MULTI RACK OVENS OR DRIVE IN CONVECTION OVENS
(Entire truck enters chambers - gas or electric - 2 or 4 rack sizes)

TYPICAL SIZES

Width	Depth	Height	Racks	Heater Location
34"	4'-10"	6'-6"	2	Rear
34"	7'-9"	7'-9"	4	Rear
34"	7'-9"	7'-9"	4	Top

TYPICAL PRODUCTION
(18" x 26" Pans - 4 Rack Oven)

	Cookies	Sheet Cakes	Pies
Per Load	1728	36	216
Rack Centers	3½"	7"	7"
Bake Time	12 min.	30 min.	35 min.
Bake Temp.	375°	375°	375°
Total Per Hr.	6,900	60-70	324

Rack is defined as mobile style 18" x 26" pan carrier constructed for this purpose and not regular tray truck style.

APPROXIMATE BAKE TIMES AND TEMPS - MULTI RACK OVENS

Product	Temp.	Time Minutes
Pizza	600°	5-8 min.
Pie	375/400°	35-50 min.
Cookies	375/400°	12 min.
Rolls	400/425°	20-30 min.
Baked Apple	300/325°	60-70 min.

Power requirements: Electric ovens, 170 KW; gas ovens, 800,000 BTU. Self-cleaning models require 1,000,000 BTU or 170 KW. Units require cold water connection and generate their own steam if required for baking.

HIGH PRODUCTION CONVECTION OVENS

Roll in dolly ovens, electric. Overall sizes: 61" wide, 31½" deep, 63" high. Available in 4 models:
1) Dual speed fan - dual power 27 and 51 KW
2) High speed fan - high heat 51 KW
3) Low speed fan - low heat 27 KW
4) Any of above models adapted for school lunch wire basket systems.

The roll in rack has a removable solid shelf plate which divides the oven into 2 separate cooking compartments and allows 2 temperature cooking if desired. Some available options to this system include solid state controls, steam injection and vent hood exhaust with motor control. Numerous shelf and grid assemblies available to match cooking requirements.

TYPICAL COOKING GUIDE FOR HIGH PRODUCTION OVENS

Sheet Pans or Racks per Oven Load	ITEM	Pounds/Pieces per Oven Load		Approximate Cooking Time Minutes
4-5	Boneless Beef Rib	280	20	130 - 150
4 - 5	Top Round of Beef	200	10	150- 165
5 - 6	Top Round Split	240	24	105 - 120
6	Bottom Round Beef	360	18	150 - 165
9 - 18	London Broil, 1"	432	216	10
8	Sirloin Strip Roast	320	32	35 - 45
6	Meat Loaf, 10½"x5½"x4"	300	50	75 - 90
9	Legs of Lamb, boned	288	72	75 - 90
9 - 18	Baked Pork Chops	135	432	20 - 25
9	Baked Chicken Halves	243	162	25 - 30
9	Baked Chicken Quarters	216	288	25 - 30
9	Barbecue Chicken Half	243	162	20 - 25
9 - 18	Sirloin Steaks	202	324	8 - 10
9 - 18	Delmonico Steaks	162	324	8 - 10
9 - 18	Salisbury Steak	169	450	18 - 22
9 - 18	Hamburgers	165	756	5 - 6
9 - 18	Fish Fillet, fresh	304	540	16 - 20

(Continued)

Sheet Pans or Racks per Oven Load	ITEM	Pounds/Pieces per Oven Load		Approximate Cooking Time Minutes
9	Fresh Fruit Pies	189	54	25 - 35
9 - 18	Cookies, varied	54	864	4 - 6
9 - 18	Sheet Cakes	108	18	25 - 35
9	*Baked Idahos	202	324	35 - 40
9	Frozen Pre-plates	34	54	25 - 30
6	Bread Dressing	120	24	25 - 35
18	Toast/English Muffins	—	432	4 - 5

*From Room Temp.

FROZEN FOOD PRODUCTS

Sheet Pans per Oven Load	ITEM	Pounds/Pieces per Oven Load		Approximate Cooking Time Minutes	Capacity (Items per pan or grid)
9	Frozen Fruit Pies, 9"x1½", on grid	189	54	45 - 50	6
9	Individual Pot Pies,				
5"x1-9/32"	79	180	25	20	
9	Casseroles, Covered,				
4¾"x1-5/8"	112	180	45	20	
9	Dinners, Individual - Covered on grids				
	9"x8½"x1"	31	54	20	6

Baskets per Oven Load					
40	School Lunch - Type A, 5"x6½" (10 pans per basket)	350	400	20	400 meals per load

Pans per Oven Load	(All on 12" x 20" Steam Table Pans)				
18	Vegetables - Covered	256	18	35 - 45	
18	Potatoes au Gratin - Covered	256	18	45	
18	Beef and Gravy Covered	256	18	45	
18	Spaghetti & Meat Balls Covered	256	18	40	
18	Shrimp Creole - Covered	256	18	40	

OVEN TEMPERATURES

Slow	250-300ºF.	Moderately Hot	400ºF
Slow-Moderate	325º	Hot	425-450ºF.
Moderate	350-375ºF.	Very Hot	475-500ºF.

GAS DECK OVENS · FACTS AND TYPICAL SIZES

Inside Deck Size	Overall Size	BTU's Per Deck
33'' x 22'' x 7'' sections	51'' x 30''	20,000
33'' x 22'' x 2-7'' sections	51'' x 30''	27,000
33'' x 22'' x 12'' sections	51'' x 30''	22,000
33'' x 22'' x 16½'' sections	51'' x 30''	27,000
42'' x 32'' x 7'' sections	60'' x 40''	37,000
42'' x 32'' x 2-7'' sections	60'' x 40''	50,000
42'' x 32'' x 12'' sections	60'' x 40''	38,000
42'' x 32'' x 16½'' sections	60'' x 40''	50,000

Using above sizes some possible combinations may be as follows:

Sections	Compartments	Sections	Compartments
1*	1 - 7'' high	1	1 - 12'' high
2	2 - 7'' high	2	2 - 12'' high
3	3 - 7'' high	2	1 - 7'' plus 1 - 12'' high
1	1 - 16¼'' high	3	2 - 7'' plus 1 - 12'' high
2	2 - 16¼'' high	1*	2 - 7'' high
2	1 - 12'' plus 1 - 16¼'' high	2*	4 - 7'' high
2*	2 - 7'' plus 1 - 16¼'' high	2*	2 - 7' plus 1 - 12'' high
2	1 - 7'' plus 1 - 16¼'' high	2*	3 - 7'' high

*These ovens have single burner compartment for 2 decks — all others have burner section for each compartment.

NOTE: Legs available in many heights to accommodate specific requirements.

DECK OVEN PAN CAPACITIES

Pan Size	DECK SIZE			
	33" x 22"	42" x 33"	37" x 54"	56" x 54"
19-¾'' x 11-7/8''	3	5	7	12
20'' x 11-1/8''	2	5	7	11
23'' x 12-5/8''	1	3	6	8
24-1/16'' x 14-1/16''	1	3	4	7
21-5/8'' x 18½''	1	2	4	6
21-13/16'' x 19-13/16	1	2	2	4
22-1/8'' x 20-1/8''	1	2	2	4
16'' x 20''	2	4	5	8
18'' x 24''	1	2	4	6
18'' x 26''	1	2	4	6
20-7/8'' x 17-3/8''	1	2	4	6

Range ovens normally hold full size 18'' x 26'' pans or smaller pans - 2 per oven.

DECK OVEN
(Suggested requirements by meals served)
12" x 20" Pan Capacity

Meals	Pan Decks Required
250	6
500	10
750	16

HELPFUL HINTS

Deck ovens for baking have a cavity height of approximately 8". Roasting and general purpose ovens have a cavity height of 11" to 16".

When considering a new oven check to see if your present pans will work well in it.

For a completely new system consider a pan flow system from storage to oven and on to serving.

CONVENTIONAL GAS OVEN TIME AND TEMPERATURE
(Guide Only)

Meats	Temperature	Time
BEEF: Ribs	325°	Rare — 16 min./lb.
		Med. — 20 min./lb.
		Well-done — 25 min./lb.
Rolled, Boneless	325°	Add 10 min./lb. to above times
Hip or Rump, Boneless	325°	30 min./lb.
VEAL: Bone-in cuts	325°	25 min./lb.
Boned cuts	325°	30 min./lb.
LAMB: Leg or shoulder	325°	35 min./lb.
Shoulder, Boned	325°	40 min./lb.
PORK: Fresh		
Bone-in cuts	350°	30-40 min./lb.
Boned cuts	350°	40-50 min./lb.
Spareribs	350°	1½ hrs./batch
PORK: Smoked	325°	16-20 min./lb.
Sliced Ham (2" thick)	325°	1½ hrs.
Picnic Hams	325°	35 min./lb.
Hams	325°	25-30 min./lb.
Bacon	350°	Depends on degree of doneness
Sausages, links, patties	350°	30 min./lb.
Frankfurters	325°	8-10 min./lb.
Meat Loaf, Ham or Beef	325°	1½ hrs.
Roast Beef Hash	350°	30-45 min./lb.
Meat Pies, deep dish	450°	12-15 min./lb.
POULTRY		
Springs	350°	15 min./lb.
Chickens, 2-3 lbs.	350°	35 min./lb.
Chickens, over 5 lbs.	325°	20-25 min./lb.
Chicken Pies	450°	15-25 min.
Turkeys, 10-16 lbs.	325°	18-20 min./lb.
Turkeys, 25 lbs.	325°	15-18 min./lb.
Turkeys, 30-35 lbs.	325°	20-25 min./lb.
Ducks		Same as Chickens
Geese		Same as Turkeys

Weights are for unstuffed birds. Stuffed, add 15 min./lb.

(Continued)

CONVENTIONAL GAS OVEN TIME AND TEMPERATURE (Cont.)
(Guide Only)

Meats	Temperature	Time
FISH		
Fish, whole	350°	15 min./lb.
Fish Fillets	350°	15-20 min./lb.
Shrimp Fondue	350°	45-60 min./lb.
Lobster	400°	Appr. 20 min./lb.
Oysters, Casino	350°	15 min.
Oysters, Devilled	350°	15 min.
Oysters, Rockefeller	450°	10 min.
Salmon Loaf	350°	45-90 min./lb.
Vegetables	**Temperature**	**Time**
BAKED		
Bananas	350°	15-20 min./lb.
Beets	350°	45-60 min./lb.
Boston Beans	250°	8 hrs.
Lima Beans	350°	Approx. 2 hrs.
Carrots	400°	Until tender
Egg Plant	350°	Until tender
Macaroni	350°	15-25 min./lb.
Mushrooms	350°	Until brown
Stuffed Peppers	350°	25 min./lb.
Potatoes	400°	75-90 min.
Spinach Loaf	325°	25 min./lb.
Tomatoes	350°	15-20 min./lb.
CHEESE		
Cheese Fondue	350°	40 min./lb.
Cheese Loaf	325°	40 min./lb.
Toasted Cheese	350°	15 min./lb.
Cheese Souffle	300°	20 min./lb.
Au gratin dishes	450°	Until browned
BAKED GOODS		
Breads: Bread, white, yeast	375-425°	30-45 min.
Raisin	400°	40 min.
Breads, rich	400°	30-45 min.
Breads, Vienna	400°	35-50 min.
Breads, rye	375°	45-90 min.
Melba toast	450-500°	Until done
Rolls:Rolls, standard white	375-400°	20-45 min.
Rolls, Parker House	400-425°	15-20 min.
Clover-leaf	400-425°	15-20 min.
Rolls, sweet dough mix	350-375°	20-40 min.
Biscuits	375-400°	15-25 min.
Danish pastry	375-400°	20-35 min.
Pies: Fresh Fruit	375-400°	50-60 min.
Pies, precooked filling	475°	20-35 min.
Pie shells	400-450°	15 min.
Pies, custard	325-450°	Depending upon filling

(Continued)

CONVENTIONAL GAS OVEN TIME AND TEMPERATURE (Cont.)
(Guide Only)

	Temperature	Time
BAKED GOODS		
Cakes: Cookies	400-475°	8-15 min.
Cheesecake, standard	350°	40 min.
Cheesecake, French	Not over 300°	1½ hrs.
Devil's Food	360-375°	20-25 min.
Fruit	300°	1½ hrs., up
White layers	350-375°	20-35 min.
Yellow layers	375°	15-25 min.
Streisel	400°	25-30 min.
DESSERTS AND PUDDINGS		
Baked Apples	400°	Approx. 1 hr.
Brown Betty	325°	45-60 min.
Fruit Pudding	375°	1 hr.
Indian Pudding	325°	3 hrs.
Miscl. Fruits	400-450°	Variable
Rice Pudding	350°	Variable

SAMPLE CAPACITIES OF DECK OVENS
(By size and product)

ELECTRIC OVENS

Deck Size: 42" wide x 32" deep

Product	Pan	No. Pans Per Deck	Produces Per Hr.
Dinner Rolls	18" x 26"	2	16-20 dz.
Layer Cake	8" Diam.	20	60
Macaroni	12" x 20"	4	960 - 4 oz. servings
Potatoes	Size varies		60-140

52" x 37" Deck

Dinner Rolls	18" x 26"	4	54 dz.
Layer Cake	8" Diam.	24	72
Macaroni	12" x 20"	6	1440 - 4 oz. servings
Potatoes	Varies		86 - 200

52" x 56" Deck

Dinner Rolls	18" x 26"	6	48 - 60 dz.
Layer Cake	8" Diam.	42	126
Macaroni	10		
Macaroni	12" x 20"	10	2400 - 4 oz. servings
Potatoes	Varies		130 - 305

TOP AND BOTTOM COOKING

Top and bottom cooking is the principle employed in electric bake ovens. Heating units are located within the baking compartment to assure utilization of all heat for thermal efficiency. And since electric ovens require no openings for the entrance of outside air to remove products of combustion, all oven sides can be uniformly insulated. Escape of heat during the baking process is reduced to minimum.

True radiant heat from the upper unit assures perfect quality control of the product top. Balanced convected heat from the lower unit assures perfect quality control of the product bottom.

Each heating unit has an area equal to approximately that of the deck and is arranged for 3-heat (low, medium, high) operation and is thermostatically controlled. This basic arrangement provides uniform heat in all size electric ovens . . . one, two and three deck.

Big advantages: less meat shrinkage and precise heat control.

HELPFUL HINTS

Allow at least 2" clearance for air circulation around pans in convection, roast or bake ovens.

CONVENTIONAL ELECTRIC TIME AND TEMPERATURE GUIDE

Product	Temperature	Top Switch	Bottom Switch	Time Minutes
Two Crust Pies	400-425	Med.	High	40-60
Open Face Pie	400-425	Med.	High	35-50
*Pumpkin Pie	375-400	Med.	Med.	35-50
*Custard Pie	375-400	Med.	Med.	35-50
Meringue Pie (browned)	425-450	High	Off	5-6
Parker House Rolls	400-425	Med.	Med.	20-30
Danish Rolls	375-400	Med.	Med.	20-30
Sweet Rolls	375-400	Med.	Med.	20-30
Tea Biscuits	375-400	Med.	Med.	20-25
Corn Bread	400-425	Med.	Med.	25-35
Layer Cake	350-375	Med.	Med.	20-30
Angel Cake	300-325	Med.	Med.	40-50
Puddings	325-375	Med.	Med.	35-60
Pizza (pre-prepared)	500	High	High	5
Pizza (fresh)	500	High	High	15

*Used when crust and filling are baked as a unit. When crust is pre-baked and filling only is to be baked, most bakers use a temperature of approximately 300-350°F.

STEAM REQUIREMENTS BY BOILER
(Horsepower Needed and Oven Type)

| EQUIPMENT | CAPACITY | BOILER HORSEPOWER | |
		Electric Oven	Gas Oven
Flat or Brick Ovens:			
Single Deck	8/12 Bun Pans	½	1
Single Deck	18/24 Bun Pans	1	1½
Single Deck	32 Bun Pans	2	3
Single Deck	42 Bun Pans	3	4
Double Deck	6/8 Bun Pans	½	1
Double Deck	12/18 Bun Pans	1	1½
Double Deck	24 Bun Pans	2	3
Double Deck	36 Bun Pans	3	4
Rotary Ovens:			
Single Deck	8 Bun Pans	1	1½
Single Deck	18 Bun Pans	1½	2
Single Deck	24 Bun Pans	2	3
Single Deck	36 Bun Pans	4	5
Double Deck	8 Bun Pans	1	2
Double Deck	12 Bun Pans	2	3
Double Deck	18 Bun Pans	3	4
Double Deck	24 Bun Pans	4	5
Revolving Ovens:			
Single Rack	12/18 Bun Pans	1½	2
Single Rack	18/24 Bun Pans	2	3
Double Rack	24/36 Bun Pans	3	4
Double Rack	36/48 Bun Pans	5	6
Proof Boxes:			
	250 Cu. Ft.	½	—
	450 Cu. Ft.	1	—
	1000 Cu. Ft.	2	—
	2600 Cu. Ft.	4	—

MICROWAVE OVENS

Another book in itself, many articles, books, and demonstrations have brought the commercial microwave to most everyone's attention. After much discussion with manufacturers, reps, and users, FEF has reduced this section to factful, useful, and hopefully easy reading. While we have covered the main points quite thoroughly FEF has two final thoughts on microwaves: 1) Read your user's manual carefully and 2) If you are planning a new operation involving microwave cooking, you may find an in-house demonstration using your specific menu items to be advantageous before final selection.

User's manuals will discuss care and cleaning procedures, utensils to be used in the oven, and specific applications. FEF will touch on food positioning, desirable design features and sample cooking guides for ovens by wattage. Wattage in microwave ovens is discussed in terms of output power.

HOW TO POSITION FOOD ON THE PLATE
FOR MICROWAVE HEATING

Several factors should be kept in mind when selecting utensils to be used for microwave heating.
1. A plate with a narrow rim of about 1/2-inch is recommended. This keeps the food all at the same level for more even, uniform heating.
2. Casseroles and sauced items should be heated in straight sided containers.
3. Containers should be chosen to be large enough to contain foods as they expand with heating. Milk products are especially subject to boil-overs.
4. Plastic, foam and paper plates should not be used when heating high fat or sugar foods such as barbecue as the heat from the fat and sugar may distort the plate.
5. Most foods heat better if they are covered. Covering retains the heat that has been created, reduces dehydration and helps keep the oven clean. There should be an opening for steam to escape from the food. Covers should also be non-metallic to allow for proper heating.
When placing foods on plate for microwave heating remember:
1. Sandwiches should be heated uncovered to prevent sogginess.
2. Sandwiches should be heated on a paper towel or napkin to absorb moisture.
3. Larger pieces of food should be placed around the outside edge of the container for best heating of casseroles or plates.
4. The center of the casserole should be slightly depressed for even heating.
5. The meat and vegetables in a casserole should be coated with sauce to reheat more easily.
6. Casseroles with crusts are the only ones that should be heated uncovered. Covering will help to speed heating of other types of casseroles.
7. Sliced meats should be at least 1/2-inch thick for best heating results. Turning the meat product over once during the heating process will yield more uniform heating.
8. The microwave oven is quite useful in reducing broiling times for steaks and chops. Partially prepare the meat in microwave oven, then broil for a shorter period of time.

HEATING AND COOKING TIME GUIDE (Cont.)
(For 650 Watt Oven)

Quantity	Item	Approximate Heating Time
3 oz.	Frankfurter	40 sec.
5 oz.	Jumbo Frankfurter	60 sec.
3½ oz.	Grilled Cheese	10 sec.
3½ oz.	Ham Sandwich	40 sec.
4 oz.	Ham & Cheese	40 sec.
5 oz.	Italian Sausage	80 sec.
4½ oz.	Pastrami	60 sec.
3½ oz.	Roast Beef	40 sec.
5½ oz.	Submarine/Hoagie	60 sec.
5 oz.	Chili Burger	60 sec.
5 oz.	Chili Dog	40 sec.
5 oz.	Sloppy Joe	60 sec.

Casseroles

Quantity	Item	Approximate Heating Time
7 oz.	Baked Beans	120 sec.
7 oz.	Beef Burgundy	120 sec.
7 oz.	Beef Goulash	120 sec.
7 oz.	Beef Stew	120 sec.
7 oz	Beef Slices w/gravy	120 sec.
7 oz.	Cabbage Rolls	120 sec.
7 oz.	Chicken Fricassee	120 sec.
7 oz.	Chicken a la King	180 sec.
7 oz.	Chili Con Carne	180 sec.
7 oz.	Creamed Chicken	120 sec.
7 oz.	Lasagna	120 sec.
7 oz.	Meat Loaf	180 sec.
7 oz.	Macaroni (beef sauce)	120 sec.
7 oz.	Macaroni (cheese sauce)	120 sec.
8 oz.	Stuffed Peppers	180 sec.
7 oz.	Pot Pie	180 sec.
7 oz.	Ravioli	180 sec.
7 oz.	Shrimp Creole	180 sec.
7 oz.	Shrimp Newburg	180 sec.
8 oz.	Short Ribs of Beef	180 sec.
7 oz.	Spaghetti	120 sec.
7 oz.	Stew, Chicken	120 sec.
7 oz.	Tuna Casserole	120 sec.
7½ oz.	Turkey Slices	180 sec.
4 oz.	Asparagus	60 sec.
4 oz.	Beans, green	60 sec.
4 oz.	Broccoli	60 sec.
4 oz.	Carrot slices	60 sec.
4 oz.	Cauliflower	40 sec.
4 oz.	Corn niblets	40 sec.
4 oz.	Mushrooms	40 sec.
4 oz.	Peas	40 sec.
4 oz.	Potatoes au gratin	60 sec.
7 oz.	Potatoes pre-baked	60 sec.

(Continued)

HEATING AND COOKING TIME GUIDE (Cont.)
(For 650 Watt Oven)

Quantity	Item	Approximate Heating Time
Defrosting		
8 oz.	Club Steak	40 on 40 off 40 on
14 oz.	Cornish Game Hen	120 on 120 off 120 on
8 oz.	Halibut Steak	40 on 40 off 40 on
8 oz.	Lamb Chops	40 on 40 off 40 on
6 oz.	Lobster Tail	40 on 40 off 40 on
8 oz.	Pork Chops	60 on 60 off 40 on
8 oz.	Salmon Steak	40 on 40 off 40 on
8 oz.	Shrimp	40 on 40 off 40 on
12 oz.	Strip Steak	40 on 40 off 40 on
10 oz.	Vegetable in pouch	60 on 60 off 40 on
Primary Cooking		
2 slices	Bacon	120 sec.
1 ear	Corn on the cob	120 sec.
5 oz.	Scrambled Eggs	120 sec.
6 oz.	Lobster Tail	180 sec.
6 oz.	Small Potato	4 min.
8 oz.	Trout	180 sec.

1000 WATT MICROWAVE
Outside dimensions 22" wide, 24¼" deep, 16" high
Inside dimensions 13¾" wide, 13¼" deep, 8½" high
Power 115-120 volts - 20 amp circuit

DESIRABLE DESIGN FEATURES:
The 1000 watt unit is recommended for moderate volume installations such as coffee shops, restaurants, diners, fast food operations and convenience stores.

IT FEATURES: 9 Computer controlled pushbuttons, easily reprogrammed and customized according to needs. Thirty-two (32) time settings from 6 seconds - 4 minutes.

10 MINUTE DIAL TIMER

TWO MAGNETRONS WITH DUAL CIRCUITRY: For greater durability and more uniform heating.

INSTANT-ON: No delay or waiting time for start up.

AUTOMATIC EDGE-CONTROL: Pulsates at 15 second on/off intervals. Eliminates overheating and crusting of edges.

COMPLETION SIGNAL: Beeps when finished.

CONCEALED ON-OFF SWITCH: Prevents unauthorized use.

ANTI-THEFT DEVICE: Provides for bolting.

SEE-THROUGH DOOR

MAGNETRON FAILURE INDICATOR LIGHT: Green light appears next to first position button.

INTERCHANGEABLE STICKER LABELS: For varying and customizing menus.

1000 WATT MICROWAVE PRODUCTION CHARTS (Cont.)

Quantity	Item	Approximate Heating Time
4-5 oz.	Bacon and Tomato	20-30 sec.
4-5 oz.	Beef Barbecue	20-30 sec.
4-5 oz.	Burger	20-30 sec.
4-5 oz.	Cheeseburger	20-30 sec.
5 oz.	Chili Burger	30-40 sec.
4 oz.	Chili Dog	20-30 sec.
4-5 oz.	Corned Beef	20-30 sec.
3 oz.	Frankfurter/Hot Dog	20 sec.
5 oz.	Frankfurter, Jumbo	20-30 sec.
3½ oz.	Grilled Cheese	20-30 sec.

DEFROSTING MEATS

8 oz.	Club Steak	90-120 sec.
8 oz.	Lamb Chops	90-120 sec.
5-6 oz.	Minute Steak	60-75 sec.
8 oz.	Pork Chops	90-120 sec.
6-8 oz.	Rib Eye Steak	90-100 sec.

Poultry

4-5 oz.	Chicken Breast, boneless	60-70 sec.
16-18 oz.	Chicken, halved	3½-4 min.
12-14 oz.	Cornish Game Hen	2½-3 min.

Seafood

12-14 oz.	Crab Legs	2½-3 min.
5-6 oz.	Fillet of Sole	70-80 sec.
5-6 oz.	Halibut Steak	70-80 sec.
6-8 oz.	Lobster Tail	80-90 sec.
6-8 oz.	Salmon Steak	80-90 sec.
6 oz.	Scallops	80-90 sec.
8 oz.	Shrimp	90-120 sec.
12-14 oz.	Stuffed Flounder	2½-3 min.
6-8 oz.	Trout	80-90 sec.

Vegetables

4 oz.	Asparagus	30-40 sec.
1 medium	Artichoke	40-50 sec.
4 oz.	Beans, green	30-40 sec.
4 oz.	Beans, lima	30-40 sec.
4 oz.	Beans, wax	30-40 sec.
4 oz.	Beets	40-50 sec.
4 oz.	Broccoli	30-40 sec.
4 oz.	Brussels Sprouts	40-50 sec.
4 oz.	Carrot Slices	40-50 sec.
4 oz.	Carrots, whole baby	50-60 sec.
4 oz.	Cauliflower	40-50 sec.
4 oz.	Corn Niblets	30-40 sec.
4 oz.	Mixed Vegetables	40-50 sec.
4 oz.	Mushrooms	20-30 sec.
4 oz.	Peas, green	20-30 sec.
4 oz.	Potatoes au gratin	40-50 sec.

(Continued)

1000 WATT MICROWAVE PRODUCTION CHARTS (Cont.)

Quantity	Item	Approximate Heating Time
4 oz.	Potatoes, mashed	50-60 sec.
4 oz.	Potatoes, prebaked	40-50 sec.
4 oz.	Spinach	30-40 sec.

Primary Cooking

Quantity	Item	Approximate Heating Time
2 strips	Bacon	80-90 sec.
6-8 strips	Bacon	3-3½ min.
1 medium	Baked Potato	3-4 min.
2 medium	Baked Potatoes	6-7 min.
3 medium	Baked Potatoes	10-11 min.
1 ear	Corn on the Cob	2-3 min.
2 ears	Corn on the Cob	5-6 min.
4 ears	Corn on the Cob	8-9 min.
5-6 oz.	Fish Fillet	1½-2 min.
6-8 oz.	Lobster Tail	2-2½ min.
2 eggs	**Scrambled Eggs**	**50-60 sec.**
6-8 oz.	**Trout**	**2-3 min.**

1400 WATT MICROWAVE

Outside dimensions 22-1/16" wide, 23-5/8" deep, 16 high
Inside dimensions 13¾" wide, 13½" deep, 7-9/16" high
Power 208/230 volts, 15 amp circuit

DESIRABLE DESIGN FEATURES:

The 1400 watt unit is recommended for high volume installations such as hospitals, restaurants, institutions and nursing homes.

IT FEATURES: 9 computer controlled pushbuttons easily reprogrammed and customized according to needs. Thirty-two (32) time settings from 6 seconds - 4 minutes.

10 MINUTE DIAL TIMER

TWO MAGNETRONS WITH DUAL CIRCUITRY: For greater durability and more uniform heating.

INSTANT-ON: No delay or waiting time for start up.

AUTOMATIC EDGE-CONTROL: Pulsates at 15 second on/off intervals. Eliminates overheating and crusting of edges.

COMPLETION SIGNAL: Beeps when finished.

CONCEALED ON-OFF SWITCH: Prevents unauthorized use.

ANTI-THEFT DEVICE: Provides for bolting.

SEE-THROUGH DOOR

MAGNETRON FAILURE INDICATOR LIGHT: Green light appears next to first position button.

INTERCHANGEABLE STICKER LABELS: For varying and customizing menus.

REMOVABLE FILTER: No tools necessary.

3 YEAR WARRANTY ON MAGNETRON TUBES

CONVEYOR PIZZA OVENS · FLOOR MODELS

Stackable decks, production per deck by tunnel length. Variable speed drive.

Pizza Style	Time	Temp.	Production Per Hr. By Tunnel Length 74"	50"	38"
5" - 12 per pan	5.5 min.	700°	372	246	130
7" Pizza	5.5 min.	700°	232	154	64
13" Thick Pizza	7 min.	650°	52	34	—
13" Thin Pizza	9 min.	675°	40	26	—
9" Deep Pizza	14 min.	575/650°	70	46	17
10" Pizza Shells	5 min.	675°	147	98	44

Also used for other breads and sandwiches.

CONVEYOR OVENS

Generally Conveyor Ovens will bake, reheat and finish food two to four times faster than Conventional Ovens. These ovens operate at lower temperatures than regular ovens and when at standby temperatures, return to the cooking temperature much faster.

SAMPLE CONVEYOR OVEN COOK TIMES AND TEMPERATURES

Product	State	Time	Top	Bottom
Nachos	Fresh	2.0	750	750
Muffins	Mix	9.0	600	600
Sandwich	Refrig.	3.0	700	700
Pizza 9"	Refrig.	4.5	750	750
Pizza 9"	Frozen	7.0	650	700
Pizza 6"	Refrig.	4.0	750	750
Garlic Bread	Refrig.	2.0	750	750
Bagels	Refrig.	1.5	750	750
Toast		1.0	750	750
English Muffins	Refrig.	2.0	800	800
Cookies	Scratch	8.0	650	650
Shrimp	Refrig.	4.1	800	800
Boneless Chicken Breast	Refrig.	5.0	800	800
Waffles	Frozen	2.0	750	750
Hot Dogs	Refrig.	3.0	750	750
Pork Chops	Refrig.	7.0	750	750
Pretzels	Frozen/Thaw	5.0	750	750
French Toast	Fresh	5.0	650	650
Hors d'Oeuvres	Refrig.	4.0	750	750
Fish Fillet	Refrig.	5.0	800	800
Ribs (finish)	Refrig.	4.0	800	800

SMOKE STYLE ROAST OVEN
(Cooks and Holds · Uses Hardwood Chips)

Size: Overall 28" wide, 29" deep, 60" high. Inside: 25" wide, 25" deep, 44" high, 208V, 3 KW plus 115V motor, slow cook capacities. Gas models also available.

Food Item	Capacity Per Load	Cook Temp.	Cook Time Hrs.
Roast Beef	200 lbs.	200°	8
1/2 Chickens	120	200°	3 1/2
Whole Chickens	60	200°	3 1/2
1" Fish Fillets	75-100	175°	3 3/4
1" Steak	75-100	200°	1 3/4
Hamburg, 4 1/2 diam.	250	200°	1 3/4
Pre-cooked Sausage	200 lbs.	175°	1 1/2
Stuffed Duck	50	180°	4

This all purpose oven roasts, holds, bakes or smokes.

INFRA RED/HICKORY SMOKER COMBINATION COOKER
(Skillet Style)

Typical Sizes and Power Requirements

	Small	Large	Product Capacity
Width	55"	69"	Small 150 lbs.
Front to Back	37"	49"	
Body Height	19"	34"	Large 300 lbs.
Overall Height	19"	34"	

Power: Small unit 5-6 KW, large unit 10-11 KW.

This unit cooks from top and bottom and has a separate wood smoking unit — smokes while it cooks. Venting only if desired.

COUNTER TOP COOKER-SMOKER

Overall size: 28 1/2" wide, 29 1/4" deep, 24" high plus legs. Power: 120 V - 1.7 KW, 14 Amp.

Cooks and smokes 80 lbs. of meat per load. Uses safe, easy liquid smoke. Completely automatic, simply set controls and switch to on. Provides efficient cooking with little shrinkage.